VOYAGEUR CLASSICS

BOOKS THAT EXPLORE CANADA

Michael Gnarowski — Series Editor

The Dundurn Group presents the Voyageur Classics series, building on the tradition of exploration and rediscovery and bringing forward time-tested writing about the Canadian experience in all its varieties.

This series of original or translated works in the fields of literature, history, politics, and biography has been gathered to enrich and illuminate our understanding of a multi-faceted Canada. Through straightforward, knowledgeable, and reader-friendly introductions, the Voyageur Classics series provides context and accessibility while breathing new life into these timeless Canadian masterpieces.

The Voyageur Classics series was designed with the widest possible readership in mind and sees a place for itself with the interested reader as well as in the classroom. Physically attractive and reset in a contemporary format, these books aim at an enlivened and updated sense of Canada's written heritage.

OTHER VOYAGEUR CLASSICS TITLES

The Blue Castle by Lucy Maud Montgomery,
introduced by Dr. Collett Tracey 978-1-55002-666-5
Canadian Exploration Literature: An Anthology,
edited and introduced by Germaine Warkentin 978-1-55002-661-0
Combat Journal for Place d'Armes: A Personal Narrative by Scott Symons, introduced by Christopher Elson 978-1-55488-457-5
The Donnellys by James Reaney, introduced by Alan Filewod 978-1-55002-832-4
Empire and Communications by Harold A. Innis,
introduced by Alexander John Watson 978-1-55002-662-7
The Firebrand: William Lyon Mackenzie and the Rebellion in Upper Canada
by William Kilbourn, introduced by Ronald Stagg 978-1-55002-800-3
In This Poem I Am: Selected Poetry of Robin Skelton,
edited and introduced by Harold Rhenisch 978-1-55002-769-3
The Letters and Journals of Simon Fraser 1806–1808, edited and introduced by
W. Kaye Lamb, foreword by Michael Gnarowski 978-1-55002-713-6
Maria Chapdelaine: A Tale of French Canada by Louis Hémon, translated by W.H.
Blake, introduction and notes by Michael Gnarowski 978-1-55002-712-9
The Men of the Last Frontier by Grey Owl,
introduced by James Polk 978-1-55488-804-7
Mrs. Simcoe's Diary by Elizabeth Posthuma Simcoe, edited and introduced
by Mary Quayle Innis, foreword by Michael Gnarowski 978-1-55002-768-6
Pilgrims of the Wild, edited and introduced by Michael Gnarowski 978-1-55488-734-7
The Refugee: Narratives of Fugitive Slaves in Canada by Benjamin Drew,
introduced by George Elliott Clarke 978-1-55002-801-0
The Scalpel, the Sword: The Story of Doctor Norman Bethune
by Ted Allan and Sydney Ostrovsky, introduced by Julie Allan,
Dr. Norman Allan, and Susan Ostrovsky 978-1-55488-402-5
Selected Writings by A.J.M. Smith,
edited and introduced by Michael Gnarowski 978-1-55002-665-8
Self Condemned by Wyndham Lewis, introduced by Allan Pero 978-1-55488-735-4
The Silence on the Shore by Hugh Garner,
introduced by George Fetherling 978-1-55488-782-8
Storm Below by Hugh Garner, introduced by Paul Stuewe 978-1-55488-456-8
A Tangled Web by Lucy Maud Montgomery,
introduced by Benjamin Lefebvre 978-1-55488-403-2
The Yellow Briar: A Story of the Irish on the Canadian Countryside
by Patrick Slater, introduced by Michael Gnarowski 978-1-55002-848-5
Duncan Campbell Scott: Selected Writings,
edited, selected, and introduced by Michael Gnarowski 978-1-45970-144-1
The Town Below by Roger Lemelin,
introduced by Michael Gnarowski 978-1-55488-803-0
Pauline Johnson: Selected Poetry and Prose by Pauline Johnson,
selected and introduced by Michael Gnarowski 978-1-45970-428-2
The Kindred of the Wild: A Book of Animal Life
by Charles G.D. Roberts, introduced by James Polk 978-1-45970-147-2
All Else Is Folly: A Tale of War and Passion by Peregrine Acland, introduced by Brian
Busby and James Calhoun, and with a preface by Ford Madox Ford 978-1-45970-423-7

VOYAGEUR CLASSICS

BOOKS THAT EXPLORE CANADA

IN FLANDERS FIELDS

AND OTHER POEMS

JOHN McCRAE

WITH AN ESSAY BY SIR ANDREW MACPHAIL
INTRODUCTION AND NOTES
BY MICHAEL GNAROWSKI

DUNDURN
TORONTO

Copyright © Dundurn, 2015
Introduction copyright © Michael Gnarowski
Originally published by The Ryerson Press

Editor: Jenny McWha
Design: Courtney Horner
Printer: Webcom
Cover designer: Jennifer Gallinger
Front cover illustration © selimaksan/iStock
All images are in the public domain.

Library and Archives Canada Cataloguing in Publication

McCrae, John, 1872-1918, author
    In Flanders fields and other poems / John McCrae ; with an essay by Sir Andrew Macphail; introduction by Michael Gnarowski.

(Voyageur classics)
Issued in print and electronic formats.
ISBN 978-1-4597-2864-6

    I. Gnarowski, Michael, 1934-, writer of introduction
II. Macphail, Andrew, Sir, 1864-1938, writer of supplementary textual content III. Title. IV. Series: Voyageur classics

PS8525.C73I5 2014   C811'.52   C2014-905031-3
                                              C2014-905032-1

1 2 3 4 5   19 18 17 16 15

We acknowledge the support of the **Canada Council for the Arts** and the **Ontario Arts Council** for our publishing program. We also acknowledge the financial support of the **Government of Canada** through the **Canada Book Fund** and **Livres Canada Books,** and the **Government of Ontario** through the **Ontario Book Publishing Tax Credit** and the **Ontario Media Development Corporation.**

Printed and bound in Canada.

VISIT US AT
Dundurn.com | *@dundurnpress* | *Facebook.com/dundurnpress* | *Pinterest.com/dundurnpress*

Dundurn
3 Church Street, Suite 500
Toronto, Ontario, Canada
M5E 1M2

CONTENTS

John McCrae.

INTRODUCTION

No piece of Canadian writing is better or more widely known than John McCrae's powerful lament cum call to arms in his poem of the First World War, "In Flanders Fields." No Canadian poem has been as widely read, admired or recited, certainly in the English-speaking world, and perhaps in the whole world itself. In whole or in part it has been memorised by children, intoned at Remembrance Day ceremonies, and has been chiselled onto rock and granite on many a cenotaph.

The author, John McCrae, the second child of David McCrae and his wife, Janet, was born on November 30, 1872, and was raised in an immigrant family of Scottish origin. Imbued with a legendary sense of thrift and hard work, and, although, relative recent arrivals — the grandfather, Thomas McCrae, landed in Canada with his family in 1849 — the McCraes displayed significant entrepreneurial ambition, so that within the span of a generation they were well-to-do residents and prominent members of the community of Guelph, Ontario. These early successes would guarantee a good education and social standing for the children.

John McCrae was schooled at the Guelph Collegiate Institute, and won a scholarship to attend the University of Toronto where he enrolled in studies leading to a Bachelor of Arts degree, although he became interested in biology and gravitated to science subjects in his second and third years. This would serve to dovetail neatly with future studies in medical school. Medicine, however, would not be his sole and exclusive life interest. As a young adolescent McCrae had served as a bugler in his father's militia artillery battery, and he would go on to maintain close ties with the militia and the artillery battery to which he had belonged in his teenage years. It was doubtless due to his father's strong sense of loyalty to the British Empire and his connections with the reserve military in Guelph that set John McCrae on his own later course of military service.

At university and in his early twenties McCrae, or Jack, as he was known to his friends, proceeded at a steady pace in his studies. Despite being divided in his interests between service in the militia, where he rose steadily to the rank of lieutenant, and having been taken under the guidance of some of the best professors of biology and zoology at the University of Toronto, Jack was clearly set on a path that would take him to a career in

John McCrae, back row left, with fellow Militia officers, 1893.

medicine. He was remembered by his friends and fellow students as an amiable, handsome young man who liked to dress well, and who had a charming personality. It is also at this point in his life that he was most active in his writing. Poems, sketches, and short stories were the by-product of this period. Having done extremely well in his studies in his undergraduate years, and now, in 1894, with his Bachelor of Arts degree in Natural Sciences, McCrae contemplated graduate studies as a next step, but a practical outlook and the advice of friends pointed him in the direction of medical studies where, for four years between 1894 and 1898, he trained to become a doctor of medicine. In the meanwhile and very much in the background, events in South Africa were heating up and leading to the second Boer War (1899–1902) into which McCrae's militia artillery unit would be drawn. McCrae went to war, and something of his South African experiences he captured in a journal, elements of which Andrew Macphail incorporated into his essay on McCrae, which appears in the prose section of this book.

Having completed his medical studies with distinction capped by a gold medal, McCrae's career prospects were excellent and opportunities soon came to him. He did a brief internship at Toronto General Hospital, then went on to intern at Johns Hopkins Hospital in Baltimore where he met and became friends with William Osler, then one of the outstanding medical professionals of his time. This experience was further enriched when McCrae moved, in late 1899, to Montreal to work at McGill University with another distinguished medical scientist of the time, J.G. Adami, with whom he would coauthor a text on pathology. At the same time it should be noted that McCrae was living through exciting times in medicine and turbulent times in the politics of the world. With the outbreak of the second Boer War, McCrae felt the pull of his other deep and abiding interest in all things military. Although there was much political debate and turmoil amongst Canadians about the war in South Africa, Canada did offer to send a contingent to help Britain's war effort on that continent. A restless and patriotically driven McCrae leaped at the chance to join a second contingent of Canadians that was assembled in late 1899, in the wake of British setbacks in the war with the Boers. In a letter that McCrae wrote to his mother it is evident that he had become a fire-breathing warrior dying to get into action, and that he was quite casual about swerving from the path of medical research in order to get into the South African War. Much to his delight, McCrae was able to join the second contingent of Canadians destined for South Africa. He was given the rank of lieutenant and placed in command of a section of artillery. The contingent sailed for the war in January of 1900, and we can judge the seriousness of the enterprise from the prose matter that Andrew Macphail has assembled for this book. It dovetails, perhaps characteristically, in the latter section with McCrae's recollections of serving "with the guns" in the Great War. Raised to the rank of major, and assailed and bedeviled by the horrors of the fighting on what can be labelled as the Flanders Front during the First World War. The dichotomy in McCrae's personality — warrior and medical man — is striking.

Upon his return from the Boer War, where he had undergone serious and strenuous campaigning and learned some valuable lessons, he concluded that the British Army was badly in need of reform. Always the independent thinker and individualist — a group photograph of his officers shows McCrae wearing a wedge cap at the rakiest angle possible while the others are all stolidly under pith helmets — the seeds of a critical outlook had been planted, and would grow and develop into a full-blown disapproval of the generalship, strategy, and tactics of the allied armies during the First World War.

McCrae returned to McGill University in 1902, taking up his fellowship in pathology while studying and working under the direction of J.G. Adami, a foremost pathologist of his time and seen, by some, as a successor influence of William Osler, the other great man of medicine who had helped shape the reputation of McGill's medical faculty. Those of McCrae's ever-growing circle of friends and professional associates who remembered him in their own letters or journals, all recalled him admiringly as a hard-working and charming individual who was much sought after as a dinner guest — not only because he was a fun-loving raconteur at the dinner table, but also because he had an inexhaustible supply of stories at the telling of which he was remarkably good and very entertaining. Proud of his looks and appearance, he affected well-tailored clothes, enjoyed Montreal society, but also thrived in the company of younger minds whose studies he helped guide. At the same time he was industrious and deadly serious about his work and duties. Andrew Macphail, the distinguished historian of medicine at McGill and friend and colleague of McCrae's, recalled the latter saying that he had never turned down any work or duty that was imposed on him, whether it was teaching or lecturing or demonstrating in the laboratory; attending the sick, doing post mortems, travelling to professional meetings or conventions or reviewing books or writing poetry. He managed it all with good humour and equal dedication. Stephen Leacock said that McCrae liked good food and drink, enjoyed his fun, disliked staying up late, and kept himself in the condition of a trained athlete

In the first decade of the twentieth century, leading up to the First World War, McCrae was deeply committed to his work as a physician and pathologist, and as a member of Montreal's social life and his circle of friends at McGill University. When the First World War began — August 4, 1914, for Canada — the Canadian military establishment of several thousand men was relatively small when compared to the large armies that the European powers could mobilise and muster for war. There was a strong patriotic feeling that swept Anglophone Canada, understandably less so in Quebec. Since the Boer War, French Canada had been reluctant to send its sons to fight what it felt were England's wars. The Anglophone ascendancy in Montreal, however, had deep military roots with well-established regiments such as the Victoria Rifles, the 17th Duke of York's Hussars, and the Black Watch as core elements upon which it could draw. The spiritual energy for these sentiments flowed from a belief in the Greater British Empire and its civilising mission, ideals to which Stephen Leacock, Andrew Macphail, and other friends of McCrae readily subscribed. Macphail, who was a self-made man who had risen to academic prominence, became in his time a foremost intellectual in Canada with ideas smudged by racism. He published much of McCrae's poetry in the *University Magazine,* of which he was editor, and was largely instrumental in keeping McCrae's memory alive after the war.

As the war had drawn nearer and the arms race between England and Germany grew ever more threatening, McCrae was beginning to enjoy the fruits of his hard work and dedication to medicine. There is evidence of his prominence in Canadian society. A canoe trip to Hudson Bay with the governor general, Lord Grey; discreet whispers of dalliance with Lady this or that; a medical conference in London attended by Willliam Osler and hosted by Lord Strathcona, all suggest a whirl of busy activity. When the war struck, McCrae, a true citizen of the British Empire, knew his duty, middle age notwithstanding, he reported to his artillery unit. The Canadian regular army being relatively few in numbers, when the call went out for volunteer recruits, men, as they liked to say, flocked to the colours. Many if not most of these soldiers-to-be were either newly arrived British immigrants or immigrants of such recent vintage that they liked to call themselves Britishers. When Hamilton Gault, a wealthy Montreal businessman, conceived the idea to create, in a near feudal gesture, a regiment for the Canadian Army, he brought into being the Princess Patricia's Canadian Light Infantry, which he funded himself and the composition of which reflected the state of affairs at Canadian recruiting stations. Of the men who joined up only a tenth were Canadian-born, the rest being British, Scots, and Irish, and many with previous experience in the British Army. They gathered at recruiting stations in gratifying numbers, and the Canadian military establishment, driven by the impetuous and intractable minister of defence, Sam Hughes, assembled some thirty thousand men and thousands of horses at Camp Valcartier, a military encampment near Quebec City, where its inadequate barracks were soon enveloped in a sea of military tents. This would form the backbone of the Canadian Expeditionary Force into which disgruntled militia units, stripped of regimental identities, were folded, the whole being transformed into an army of presumably characterless numbered battalions.

As the elements of what was to become the First Canadian Division were being assembled, McCrae was raised to the rank of major and appointed brigade-surgeon and second in command of the artillery brigade to which he had been assigned. All the while and true to his instincts, McCrae clung steadfastly to his role as a combatant, rarely seeing himself as a medical officer. On October 3, the contingent sailed from Canada with some thirty thousand officers and men and several thousand horses, all crammed into thirty-three transport ships that were also carrying arms, ammunition, and related equipment. The men fully expected to land in France and go directly into action. Instead they landed in Plymouth, were welcomed by cheering crowds, and moved to Salisbury Plain into tents which, when the weather turned, soon became a nightmare of a cold and damp existence. In addition, British military brass was not exactly chuffed at their arrival. They were seen as "colonial troops" with poor training and lax discipline. Particularly irksome to the British toffee-nosed officers was the lack of deference and awareness of class and place shown by this rabble which, while they may not have read Alexander MacLachlan's Canadian poem, clearly believed, as he had, that "jack was as good as his Master." The Canadians were also surprised and irked at how many able-bodied men they saw in civilian clothes on the streets, as well as being annoyed at reports of strikes for more pay during a war, thuggish merchants who overcharged, and unfriendly pub owners who saw the Canadians as prone to starting brawls.

The disgruntled and rain-sodden Canadians were finally dispatched to the front, arriving in the opening months of 1915. They were immediately thrown into the worst battles of the war, beginning with the gas attack at Ypres and the to-and-fro struggles for the useless salients that both sides tried to push into the enemies' lines. A great disillusionment and sadness set in on McCrae, and in March of 1915 he was writing to his mother to tell her that the makeshift burial grounds around the battlefields of Flanders, the cemeteries where the poppies of his famous poem were destined to bloom, were rapidly filling up. We can get a worm's eye view of those times from the excerpted passages that Andrew Macphail had assembled in the "With the Guns" section of this book. As a matter of fact the most telling events of McCrae's war were beginning to unfold. On May 2, the chaplain being unavailable, McCrae was called upon to read the service during the burial of what little remained of his close friend Alexis Helmer, who had been killed earlier that day by a German shell. McCrae had known Helmer in Montreal and in spite of a significant (some fifteen years) age difference the two had become close friends. Helmer, the son of a prominent family (his father had been a brigadier-general) was a graduate of the Royal Military College and of McGill University. He had belonged to the kind of elite circles to which McCrae had been happily drawn. McCrae himself had been very much a squire in the making as he went to war. He had been given the gift of his own horse before leaving for the war, which he named Bonfire, and on which he would canter for exercise behind the lines; he had his own dog, Bonneau, to which he was equally attached, and, of course, as an officer of rank, he had a man servant (or "batman," as they were commonly designated) who looked after his quarters and his needs. Going to war with old friends at your side was the slightly old-fashioned social key, and besides Helmer there was his commanding officer, Colonel Morrison, and others whom Jack had known since his days of service in the Boer War.

Helmer, of course, is particularly important since it is his death that reportedly had devastated and prompted McCrae to write his iconic poem, which appeared anonymously in the December 8, 1915, issue of *Punch*, a foremost British periodical of the day.

Up to the middle of 1915, McCrae had been more artillery man than medical doctor, but in June, with mounting casualties and a shortage of doctors, he was posted to the newly formed 3rd Canadian General Hospital. This facility, an initiative of McGill University, was made as an offer that had been carried to the British authorities by no less a figure than Sir William Osler, who had been knighted in 1911. The offer having been warmly accepted McCrae, now raised in rank to lieutenant-colonel, was appointed chief of medicine at the facility. Pulled back from the front lines, he went to England for some leave before reporting, in mid June of 1915, to Number 3 Canadian Hospital located at Dannes-Camiers, not far from the transit and embarkation port of Boulogne. McCrae would not be spared the agony of casualties in the thousands that streamed back to the military hospitals and ambulance units from the horrific batttles (Loos, Ypres, Somme) of 1916 and 1917, all of which — and in spite of their intensity of action and great loss of human life — were grinding toward what would, essentially, become a stalemate on the battlefield.

Lieutenant Alexis Hannum Helmer, First Brigade, Canadian Field Artillery. Killed in action May 2, 1915, aged twenty-two years.

For McCrae personally, the period between 1915 and early 1918 was one of great overwork, a growing sense of futility and depression about the war, and a gradual deterioration of health, brought on by worsening and debilitating attacks of asthma. Late in January of 1918, McCrae was honoured with his appointment as consulting physician to the First British Army, but he was in a poor physical state and a short time later his health broke. He was moved to the British General Hospital for Officers where, on January 28, he succumbed to a combination of pneumonia and meningitis. McCrae was buried two days later with full military honours; his horse, Bonfire, led the funeral procession with McCrae's boots reversed in the stirrups. The funeral was attended by many friends and senior officers including Sir Arthur Currie, commander of the Canadian Corps.

When we read the poems that Andrew Macphail — later Sir Andrew because he was knighted after the war for his services — gathered for this volume and which are a good representation of McCrae the poet, we come away with the feeling that he was not the kind of war poet that Wilfred Owen, Siegfried Sassoon, or Isaac Rosenberg turned out to be. Disturbed by the war and its tragic unfolding, McCrae, perhaps because he had not had the infantry soldier's experience of trench warfare, did not work up the anger and real-life responses of someone who had gone "over the top," heard the machine gun's rattle at his ear, and had seen his comrades fall and die like cattle. He was a late-nineteenth-century man who had lived twenty-nine years of his life in Victorian times, and he carried with him the poetic sentiments of that age. Modernism did not take hold of him the way it did many of his contemporaries, and McCrae remained faithful to the ideals of an earlier and seemingly nobler age.

Michael Gnarowski
August 4, 2014

RELATED READING

Tim Cook's two-volume history, *At the Sharp End* (2007) and *Shock Troops* (2008) of Canadians in the First World War is invaluable.

Lyn Macdonald in her book *1915:The Death of Innocence* (1993) provides a sharp picture of the events of 1915, a watershed year in the Great War; and John F. Prescott in his *In Flanders Fields:The Story of John McCrae* (1985) gives us important insights into the life and character of John McCrae.

A NOTE ON THE TEXT

*I*n *Flanders Fields and Other Poems* was first issued in 1919 under the imprint of William Briggs in Toronto. William Briggs (1835–1922) was an Irish immigrant and an ordained minister in the Methodist Church of Canada. He was named book steward of the Methodist Book and Publishing House in 1879. It was changed to The Ryerson Press in 1920, the imprint under which later editions of *In Flanders Fields* were issued. G.P. Putnam's Sons published the American edition.

In Flanders Fields

And Other Poems

By

Lieut.-Col. John McCrae, M.D.

With

An Essay in Character

By

Sir Andrew Macphail

ILLUSTRATED

Toronto
THE RYERSON PRESS
1920

Title page from the 1920 version of In Flanders Fields and Other Poems.

PART 1

IN FLANDERS FIELDS
AND OTHER POEMS

NOTE OF
ACKNOWLEDGEMENT

Acknowledgement and thanks are due to the following for permission to use poems: Toronto *Varsity*; *Canadian Magazine*; *Massey's Magazine*; *Westminster*; Toronto *Globe*; *The University Magazine*; *Punch*; and *The Spectator*.

The reproduction of the autograph poem is from a copy belonging to Carleton Noyes, Esq., of Cambridge, Mass., who kindly permitted its use.

Facsimile of an autograph copy of the poem "In Flanders Fields." This was probably written from memory, as "grow" is used in place of "blow" in the first line.

IN FLANDERS FIELDS

In Flanders fields the poppies blow
Between the crosses, row on row,
    That mark our place; and in the sky
    The larks, still bravely singing, fly
Scarce heard amid the guns below.

We are the Dead. Short days ago
We lived, felt dawn, saw sunset glow,
    Loved and were loved, and now we lie,
        In Flanders fields.

Take up our quarrel with the foe:
To you from failing hands we throw
The torch; be yours to hold it high.
    If ye break faith with us who die
    We shall not sleep, though poppies grow
        In Flanders fields.

THE ANXIOUS DEAD

O guns, fall silent till the dead men hear
    Above their heads the legions pressing on:
(These fought their fight in time of bitter fear,
    And died not knowing how the day had gone.)

O flashing muzzles, pause, and let them see
    The coming dawn that streaks the sky afar;
Then let your mighty chorus witness be
    To them, and Cæsar, that we still make war.

Tell them, O guns, that we have heard their call,
    That we have sworn, and will not turn aside,
That we will onward till we win or fall,
    That we will keep the faith for which they died.

Bid them be patient, and some day, anon,
    They shall feel earth enwrapt in silence deep;
Shall greet, in wonderment, the quiet dawn,
    And in content may turn them to their sleep.

THE WARRIOR

He wrought in poverty, the dull grey days,
    But with the night his little lamp-lit room
Was bright with battle flame, or through a haze
    Of smoke that stung his eyes he heard the boom
Of Blücher's guns; he shared Almeida's scars,
    And from the close-packed deck, about to die,
Looked up and saw the *Birkenhead*'s tall spars
    Weave wavering lines across the Southern sky:

Or in the stifling 'tween decks, row on row,
    At Aboukir, saw how the dead men lay;
Charged with the fiercest in Busaco's strife,
Brave dreams are his — the flick'ring lamp burns low —
Yet couraged for the battles of the day
    He goes to stand full face to face with life.

ISANDLWANA[1]

Scarlet coats, and crash o' the band,
    The grey of a pauper's gown,
    A soldier's grave in Zululand,
And a woman in Brecon Town.

My little lad for a soldier boy,
    (Mothers o' Brecon Town!)
My eyes for tears and his for joy
    When he went from Brecon Town,
His for the flags and the gallant sights
His for the medals and his for the fights,
And mine for the dreary, rainy nights
    At home in Brecon Town.

They say he's laid beneath a tree,
    (Come back to Brecon Town!)
Shouldn't I know? — I was there to see:
    (It's far to Brecon Town!)
It's me that keeps it trim and drest
With a briar there and a rose by his breast —
The English flowers he likes the best
    That I bring from Brecon Town.

And I sit beside him — him and me,
    (We're back to Brecon Town.)
To talk of the things that used to be
    (Grey ghosts of Brecon Town);
I know the look o' the land and sky,
And the bird that builds in the tree near by,
And times I hear the jackals cry,
    And me in Brecon Town.

Golden grey on miles of sand
    The dawn comes creeping down;
It's day in far off Zululand
    And night in Brecon Town.

THE UNCONQUERED DEAD

"... defeated, with great loss."

Not we the conquered! Not to us the blame
  Of them that flee, of them that basely yield;
  Nor ours the shout of victory, the fame
Of them that vanquish in a stricken field.

That day of battle in the dusty heat
  We lay and heard the bullets swish and sing
Like scythes amid the over-ripened wheat,
  And we the harvest of their garnering.

Some yielded, No, not we! Not we, we swear
  By these our wounds; this trench upon the hill
Where all the shell-strewn earth is seamed and bare,
  Was ours to keep; and lo! we have it still.

We might have yielded, even we, but death
  Came for our helper; like a sudden flood
The crashing darkness fell; our painful breath
  We drew with gasps amid the choking blood.

The roar fell faint and farther off, and soon
　　Sank to a foolish humming in our ears,
Like crickets in the long, hot afternoon
　　Among the wheat fields of the olden years.

Before our eyes a boundless wall of red
　　Shot through by sudden streaks of jagged pain!
Then a slow-gathering darkness overhead
　　And rest came on us like a quiet rain.

Not we the conquered! Not to us the shame,
　　Who hold our earthen ramparts, nor shall cease
To hold them ever; victors we, who came
　　In that fierce moment to our honoured peace.

THE CAPTAIN
1797

Here all the day she swings from tide to tide,
  Here all night long she tugs a rusted chain,
A masterless hulk that was a ship of pride,
  Yet unashamed: her memories remain.

It was Nelson in the *Captain*, Cape St.Vincent far alee,
  With the *Vanguard* leading s'uth'ard in the haze —
Little Jervis and the Spaniards and the fight that was to be,
Twenty-seven Spanish battleships, great bullies of the sea,
  And the *Captain* there to find her day of days.

Right into them the *Vanguard* leads, but with a sudden tack
  The Spaniards double swiftly on their trail;
Now Jervis overshoots his mark, like some too eager pack,
He will not overtake them, haste he e'er so greatly back,
  But Nelson and the *Captain* will not fail.

Like a tigress on her quarry leaps the *Captain* from her place,
  To lie across the fleeing squadron's way:
Heavy odds and heavy onslaught, gun to gun and face to face,
Win the ship a name of glory, win the men a death of grace,
  For a little hold the Spanish fleet in play.

Ended now the *Captain's* battle, stricken sore she falls aside
　Holding still her foemen, beaten to the knee:
As the *Vanguard* drifted past her, "Well done, *Captain*," Jervis cried,
Rang the cheers of men that conquered, ran the blood of men
that died,
　And the ship had won her immortality.

Lo! here her progeny of steel and steam,
　A funnelled monster at her mooring swings:
Still, in our hearts, we see her pennant stream,
　And "Well done, Captain," like a trumpet rings.

THE SONG OF THE DERELICT

Ye have sung me your songs, ye have chanted your rimes
    (I scorn your beguiling, O sea!)
Ye fondle me now, but to strike me betimes.
    (A treacherous lover, the sea!)
Once I saw as I lay, half-awash in the night
A hull in the gloom — a quick hail — and a light
And I lurched o'er to leeward and saved her for spite
    From the doom that ye meted to me.

I was sister to *Terrible*, seventy-four,
    (Yo ho! for the swing of the sea!)
And ye sank her in fathoms a thousand or more
    (Alas! for the might of the sea!)
Ye taunt me and sing me her fate for a sign!
What harm can ye wreak more on me or on mine?
Ho braggart! I care not for boasting of thine —
    A fig for the wrath of the sea!

Some night to the lee of the land I shall steal,
   (Heigh-ho to be home from the sea!)
No pilot but Death at the rudderless wheel,
   (None knoweth the harbor as he!)
To lie where the slow tide creeps hither and fro
And the shifting sand laps me around, for I know
That my gallant old crew are in Port long ago —
   For ever at peace with the sea!

QUEBEC
1608–1908

Of old, like Helen, guerdon of the strong —
   Like Helen fair, like Helen light of word, —
"The spoils unto the conquerors belong.
   Who winneth me must win me by the sword."

Grown old, like Helen, once the jealous prize
   That strong men battled for in savage hate,
Can she look forth with unregretful eyes,
   Where sleep Montcalm and Wolfe beside her gate?

THEN AND NOW

Beneath her window in the fragrant night
  I half forget how truant years have flown
Since I looked up to see her chamber-light,
  Or catch, perchance, her slender shadow thrown
Upon the casement; but the nodding leaves
  Sweep lazily across the unlit pane,
And to and fro beneath the shadowy eaves,
  Like restless birds, the breath of coming rain
Creeps, lilac-laden, up the village street
  When all is still, as if the very trees
Were listening for the coming of her feet
  That come no more; yet, lest I weep, the breeze
Sings some forgotten song of those old years
Until my heart grows far too glad for tears.

UNSOLVED

Amid my books I lived the hurrying years,
　Disdaining kinship with my fellow man;
Alike to me were human smiles and tears,
　I cared not whither Earth's great life-stream ran,
Till as I knelt before my mouldered shrine,
　God made me look into a woman's eyes;
And I, who thought all earthly wisdom mine,
　Knew in a moment that the eternal skies
Were measured but in inches, to the quest
　That lay before me in that mystic gaze.
"Surely I have been errant: it is best
　That I should tread, with men their human ways."
God took the teacher, ere the task was learned,
And to my lonely books again I turned.

THE HOPE OF MY HEART

"*Delicta juventutis et ignorantius ejus, quoesumus ne memineris, Domine.*"

I left, to earth, a little maiden fair,
  With locks of gold, and eyes that shamed the light;
I prayed that God might have her in His care
    And sight.

Earth's love was false; her voice, a siren's song;
  (Sweet mother-earth was but a lying name)
The path she showed was but the path of wrong
    And shame.

"Cast her not out!" I cry. God's kind words come —
  "Her future is with Me, as was her past;
It shall be My good will to bring her home
    At last."

PENANCE

My lover died a century ago,
Her dear heart stricken by my sland'rous breath,
Wherefore the Gods forbade that I should know
    The peace of death.

Men pass my grave, and say, "'Twere well to sleep,
Like such an one, amid the uncaring dead!"
How should they know the vigils that I keep,
    The tears I shed?

Upon the grave, I count with lifeless breath,
Each night, each year, the flowers that bloom and die,
Deeming the leaves, that fall to dreamless death,
    More blest than I.

'Twas just last year — I heard two lovers pass
So near, I caught the tender words he said:
To-night the rain-drenched breezes sway the grass
    Above his head.

That night full envious of his life was I,
That youth and love should stand at his behest;
To-night, I envy him, that he should lie
    At utter rest.

SLUMBER SONGS

I

Sleep, little eyes
That brim with childish tears amid thy play,
Be comforted! No grief of night can weigh
Against the joys that throng thy coming day.

Sleep, little heart!
There is no place in Slumberland for tears:
Life soon enough will bring its chilling fears
And sorrows that will dim the after years.
Sleep, little heart!

II

Ah, little eyes
Dead blossoms of a springtime long ago,
That life's storm crushed and left to lie below
The benediction of the falling snow!

Sleep, little heart
That ceased so long ago its frantic beat!
The years that come and go with silent feet
Have naught to tell save this — that rest is sweet.
Dear little heart.

THE OLDEST DRAMA

"It fell on a day, that he went out to his father to the reapers.
And he said unto his father, My head, my head. And he said
to a lad, Carry him to his mother. And ... he sat on her knees
till noon, and then died. And she went up, and laid him on
the bed,... And shut the door upon him and went out."

Immortal story that no mother's heart
    Ev'n yet can read, nor feel the biting pain
That rent her soul! Immortal not by art
    Which makes a long past sorrow sting again

Like grief of yesterday: but since it said
    In simplest word the truth which all may see,
Where any mother sobs above her dead
    And plays anew the silent tragedy.

RECOMPENSE

I saw two sowers in Life's field at morn,
    To whom came one in angel guise and said,
"Is it for labour that a man is born?
    "Lo: I am Ease. Come ye and eat my bread!"
Then gladly one forsook his task undone
    And with the Tempter went his slothful way,
The other toiled until the setting sun
    With stealing shadows blurred the dusty day.

Ere harvest time, upon earth's peaceful breast
    Each laid him down among the unreaping dead.
"Labour hath other recompense than rest,
    Else were the toiler like the fool," I said;
"God meteth him not less, but rather more
Because he sowed and others reaped his store."

MINE HOST

There stands a hostel by a travelled way;
    Life is the road and Death the worthy host;
Each guest he greets, nor ever lacks to say,
    "How have ye fared?" They answer him, the most,
"This lodging place is other than we sought;
    We had intended farther, but the gloom
Came on apace, and found us ere we thought:
    Yet will we lodge. Thou hast abundant room."

Within sit haggard men that speak no word,
    No fire gleams their cheerful welcome shed;
No voice of fellowship or strife is heard
    But silence of a multitude of dead.
"Naught can I offer ye," quoth Death, "but rest!"
    And to his chamber leads each tired guest.

EQUALITY

I saw a King, who spent his life to weave
    Into a nation all his great heart thought,
Unsatisfied until he should achieve
    The grand ideal that his manhood sought;
Yet as he saw the end within his reach,
    Death took the sceptre from his failing hand,
And all men said, "He gave his life to teach
    The task of honour to a sordid land!"
Within his gates I saw, through all those years,
    One at his humble toil with cheery face,
Whom (being dead) the children, half in tears,
    Remembered oft, and missed him from his place.
If he be greater that his people blessed
Than he the children loved, God knoweth best.

ANARCHY

I saw a city filled with lust and shame,
   Where men, like wolves, slunk through the grim half-light;
And sudden, in the midst of it, there came
   One who spoke boldly for the cause of Right.

And speaking, fell before that brutish race
   Like some poor wren that shrieking eagles tear,
While brute Dishonour, with her bloodless face
   Stood by and smote his lips that moved in prayer.

"Speak not of God! In centuries that word
   Hath not been uttered! Our own king are we."
And God stretched forth his finger as He heard
   And o'er it cast a thousand leagues of sea.

DISARMAMENT

One spake amid the nations, "Let us cease
　　From darkening with strife the fair World's light,
We who are great in war be great in peace.
　　No longer let us plead the cause by might."

But from a million British graves took birth
　　A silent voice — the million spake as one —
"If ye have righted all the wrongs of earth
　　Lay by the sword! Its work and ours is done."

THE DEAD MASTER

Amid earth's vagrant noises, he caught the note sublime:
   To-day around him surges from the silences of Time
A flood of nobler music, like a river deep and broad,
   Fit song for heroes gathered in the banquet-hall of God.

THE HARVEST OF THE SEA

The earth grows white with harvest; all day long
   The sickles gleam, until the darkness weaves
Her web of silence o'er the thankful song
   Of reapers bringing home the golden sheaves.

The wave tops whiten on the sea fields drear,
   And men go forth at haggard dawn to reap;
But ever 'mid the gleaners' song we hear
   The half-hushed sobbing of the hearts that weep.

THE DYING OF PÈRE PIERRE

"... *with two other priests; the same night he died, and was*
buried by the shores of the lake that bears his name."
— Chronicle

"Nay, grieve not that ye can no honour give
    To these poor bones that presently must be
But carrion; since I have sought to live
    Upon God's earth, as He hath guided me,
I shall not lack! Where would ye have me lie?
    High heaven is higher than cathedral nave:
Do men paint chancels fairer than the sky?"
    Beside the darkened lake they made his grave,
Below the altar of the hills; and night
    Swung incense clouds of mist in creeping lines
That twisted through the tree-trunks, where the light
    Groped through the arches of the silent pines:
And he, beside the lonely path he trod,
Lay, tombed in splendour, in the House of God.

EVENTIDE

The day is past and the toilers cease;
The land grows dim 'mid the shadows grey,
And hearts are glad, for the dark brings peace
    At the close of day.

Each weary toiler, with lingering pace,
As he homeward turns, with the long day done,
Looks out to the west, with the light on his face
    Of the setting sun.

Yet some see not (with their sin-dimmed eyes)
The promise of rest in the fading light;
But the clouds loom dark in the angry skies
    At the fall of night.

And some see only a golden sky
Where the elms their welcoming arms stretch wide
To the calling rooks, as they homeward fly
    At the eventide.

It speaks of peace that comes after strife,
Of the rest He sends to the hearts He tried,
Of the calm that follows the stormiest life —
    God's eventide.

UPON WATTS' PICTURE "SIC TRANSIT"[2]

"What I spent I had; what I saved, I lost; what I gave, I have."

But yesterday the tourney, all the eager joy of life,
    The waving of the banners, and the rattle of the spears,
The clash of sword and harness, and the madness of the strife;
    To-night begin the silence and the peace of endless years.

    (*One sings within.*)

But yesterday the glory and the prize,
    And best of all, to lay it at her feet,
To find my guerdon in her speaking eyes:
    I grudge them not, — they pass, albeit sweet.

The ring of spears, the winning of the fight,
    The careless song, the cup, the love of friends,
The earth in spring — to live, to feel the light —
    'Twas good the while it lasted: here it ends.

Remain the well-wrought deed in honour done,
    The dole for Christ's dear sake, the words that fall
In kindliness upon some outcast one, —
    They seemed so little: now they are my All.

A SONG OF COMFORT

"Sleep, weary ones, while ye may — Sleep, oh, sleep!"
— Eugene Field

Thro' May time blossoms, with whisper low,
The soft wind sang to the dead below:
"Think not with regret on the Springtime's song
And the task ye left while your hands were strong.
The song would have ceased when the Spring was past,
And the task that was joyous be weary at last."

To the winter sky when the nights were long
The tree-tops tossed with a ceaseless song:
"Do ye think with regret on the sunny days
And the path ye left, with its untrod ways?
The sun might sink in a storm cloud's frown
And the path grow rough when the night came down."

In the grey twilight of the autumn eves,
It sighed as it sang through the dying leaves:
"Ye think with regret that the world was bright,
That your path was short and your task was light;
The path, though short, was perhaps the best
And the toil was sweet, that it led to rest."

THE PILGRIMS

An uphill path, sun-gleams between the showers,
   Where every beam that broke the leaden sky
Lit other hills with fairer ways than ours;
   Some clustered graves where half our memories lie;
And one grim Shadow creeping ever nigh:
      And this was Life.

Wherein we did another's burden seek,
   The tired feet we helped upon the road,
The hand we gave the weary and the weak,
   The miles we lightened one another's load,
When, faint to falling, onward yet we strode:
      This too was Life.

Till, at the upland, as we turned to go
   Amid fair meadows, dusky in the night,
The mists fell back upon the road below;
   Broke on our tired eyes the western light;
The very graves were for a moment bright:
      And this was Death.

THE SHADOW OF THE CROSS

At the drowsy dusk when the shadows creep
From the golden west, where the sun-beams sleep,

An angel mused: "Is there good or ill
In the mad world's heart, since on Calvary's hill

'Round the cross a mid-day twilight fell
That darkened earth and o'ershadowed hell?"

Through the streets of a city the angel sped;
Like an open scroll men's hearts he read.

In a monarch's ear his courtiers lied
And humble faces hid hearts of pride.

Men's hate waxed hot, and their hearts grew cold,
As they haggled and fought for the lust of gold.

Despairing, he cried, "After all these years
Is there naught but hatred and strife and tears?"

He found two waifs in an attic bare;
— A single crust was their meagre fare —

One strove to quiet the other's cries,
And the love-light dawned in her famished eyes

As she kissed the child with a motherly air:
"I don't need mine, you can have my share."

Then the angel knew that the earthly cross
And the sorrow and shame were not wholly loss.

At dawn, when hushed was earth's busy hum
And men looked not for their Christ to come,

From the attic poor to the palace grand,
The King and the beggar went hand in hand.

THE NIGHT COMETH

Cometh the night. The wind falls low,
The trees swing slowly to and fro:
   Around the church the headstones grey
   Cluster, like children strayed away
But found again, and folded so.

No chiding look doth she bestow:
If she is glad, they cannot know;
   If ill or well they spend their day,
     Cometh the night.

Singing or sad, intent they go;
They do not see the shadows grow;
   "There yet is time," they lightly say,
   "Before our work aside we lay";
Their task is but half-done, and lo!
     Cometh the night.

IN DUE SEASON

If night should come and find me at my toil,
    When all Life's day I had, tho' faintly, wrought,
And shallow furrows, cleft in stony soil
    Were all my labour: Shall I count it naught

If only one poor gleaner, weak of hand,
    Shall pick a scanty sheaf where I have sown?
"Nay, for of thee the Master doth demand
    Thy work: the harvest rests with Him alone."

PART 2

JOHN McCRAE

An Essay in Character
SIR ANDREW MACPHAIL[3]

JOHN McCRAE

I
In Flanders Fields

"In Flanders Fields," the piece of verse from which this little book takes its title, first appeared in *Punch* in the issue of December 8th, 1915. At the time I was living in Flanders at a convent in front of Locre, in shelter of Kemmel Hill, which lies seven miles south and slightly west of Ypres. The piece bore no signature, but it was unmistakably from the hand of John McCrae.

From this convent of women which was the headquarters of the 6th Canadian Field Ambulance, I wrote to John McCrae, who was then at Boulogne, accusing him of the authorship, and furnished him with evidence. From memory — since at the front one carries one book only — I quoted to him another piece of his own verse, entitled "The Night Cometh":

"Cometh the night. The wind falls low,
The trees swing slowly to and fro;
Around the church the headstones grey
Cluster, like children stray'd away,
But found again, and folded so."

It will be observed at once by reference to the text that in form the two poems are identical. They contain the same number of lines and feet as surely all sonnets do. Each travels upon two rhymes with the members of a broken couplet in widely separated refrain. To the casual reader this much is obvious, but there are many subtleties in the verse which made the authorship inevitable. It was a form upon which he had worked for years, and made his own. When the moment arrived the medium was ready. No other medium could have so well conveyed the thought.

This familiarity with his verse was not a matter of accident. For many years I was editor of the *University Magazine*, and those who are curious about such things may discover that one half of the poems contained in this little book were first published upon its pages. This magazine had its origin in McGill University, Montreal, in the year 1902. Four years later its borders were enlarged to the wider term, and it strove to express an educated opinion upon questions immediately concerning Canada, and to treat freely in a literary way all matters which have to do with politics, industry, philosophy, science, and art.

To this magazine during those years John McCrae contributed all his verse. It was therefore not unseemly that I should have written to him, when "In Flanders Fields" appeared in *Punch*. Amongst his papers I find my poor letter, and many others of which something more might be made if one were concerned merely with the literary side of his life rather than with his life itself. Two references will be enough. Early in 1905 he offered "The Pilgrims" for publication. I notified him of the place assigned to it in the magazine, and added a few words of appreciation, and after all these years it has come back to me.

The letter is dated February 9th, 1905, and reads: "I place the poem next to my own buffoonery. It is the real stuff of poetry. How did you make it? What have you to do with medicine? I was charmed with it: the thought high, the image perfect, the expression complete; not too reticent, not too full. *Videntes autem stellam gavisi sunt gaudio magno valde.* In our own tongue, —'*slainte filidh.*'"To his mother he wrote,"the Latin is translatable as,'seeing the star they rejoiced with exceeding gladness.'" For the benefit of those whose education has proceeded no further than the Latin, it may be explained that the two last words mean,"Hail to the poet."

To the inexperienced there is something portentous about an appearance in print and something mysterious about the business of an editor. A legend has already grown up around the publication of"In Flanders Fields" in *Punch.* The truth is,"that the poem was offered in the usual way and accepted; that is all." The usual way of offering a piece to an editor is to put it in an envelope with a postage stamp outside to carry it there, and a stamp inside to carry it back. Nothing else helps.

An editor is merely a man who knows his right hand from his left, good from evil, having the honesty of a kitchen cook who will not spoil his confection by favour for a friend. Fear of a foe is not a temptation, since editors are too humble and harmless to have any. There are of course certain slight offices which an editor can render, especially to those whose writings he does not intend to print, but John McCrae required none of these. His work was finished to the last point. He would bring his piece in his hand and put it on the table. A wise editor knows when to keep his mouth shut; but now I am free to say that he never understood the nicety of the semi-colon, and his writing was too heavily stopped.

He was not of those who might say, — take it or leave it; but rather, — look how perfect it is; and it was so. Also he was the first to recognize that an editor has some rights and prejudices, that certain words make him sick; that certain other words he reserves for his own use, — "meticulous" once a year, "adscititious" once in a life time. This explains why editors write so little. In the end, out of mere good nature, or seeing the futility of it all, they contribute their words to contributors and write no more.

The volume of verse as here printed is small. The volume might be enlarged; it would not be improved. To estimate the value and institute a comparison of those herein set forth would be a congenial but useless task, which may well be left to those whose profession it is to offer instruction to the young. To say that "In Flanders Fields" is not the best would involve one in controversy. It did give expression to a mood which at the time was universal, and will remain as a permanent record when the mood is passed away.

The poem was first called to my attention by a Sapper officer, then Major, now Brigadier. He brought the paper in his hand from his billet in Dranoutre. It was printed on page 468, and Mr. *Punch* will be glad to be told that, in his annual index, in the issue of December 29th, 1915, he has misspelled the author's name, which is perhaps the only mistake he ever made. This officer could himself weave the sonnet with deft fingers, and he pointed out many deep things. It is to the sappers the army always goes for "technical material."

The poem, he explained, consists of thirteen lines in iambic tetrameter and two lines of two iambics each; in all, one line more than the sonnet's count. There are two rhymes only, since the short lines must be considered blank, and are, in fact, identical. But it is a difficult mode. It is true, he allowed, that the octet of the sonnet has only two rhymes, but these recur only four times, and the liberty of the sestet tempers its despotism, — which I thought a pretty phrase. He pointed out the dangers inherent in a restricted rhyme, and cited the case of Browning, the great rhymster, who was prone to resort to any rhyme, and frequently ended in absurdity, finding it easier to make a new verse than to make an end.

At great length — but the December evenings in Flanders are long, how long, O Lord! — this Sapper officer demonstrated the skill with which the rhymes are chosen. They are vocalized. Consonant endings would spoil the whole effect. They reiterate O and I, not the O of pain and the Ay of assent, but the O of wonder, of hope, of aspiration; and the I of personal pride, of jealous immortality, of the Ego against the Universe. They are, he went on to expound, a recurrence of the ancient question: "How are the dead raised, and with what body do they come?" "How shall I bear my light across?" and of the defiant cry: "If Christ be not raised, then is our faith vain."

The theme has three phases: the first a calm, a deadly calm, opening statement in five lines; the second in four lines, an explanation, a regret, a reiteration of the first; the third, without preliminary crescendo, breaking out into passionate adjuration in vivid metaphor, a poignant appeal which is at once a blessing and a curse. In the closing line is a satisfying return to the first phase, — and the thing is done. One is so often reminded of the poverty of men's invention, their best being so incomplete, their greatest so trivial, that one welcomes what — this Sapper officer surmised — may become a new and fixed mode of expression in verse.

As to the theme itself — I am using his words: what is his is mine; what is mine is his — the interest is universal. The dead, still conscious, fallen in a noble cause, see their graves overblown in a riot of poppy bloom. The poppy is the emblem of sleep. The dead desire to sleep undisturbed, but yet curiously take an interest in passing events. They regret that they have not been permitted to live out their life to its normal end. They call on the living to finish their task, else they shall not sink into that complete repose which they desire, in spite of the balm of the poppy. Formalists may protest that the poet is not sincere, since it is the seed and not the flower that produces sleep. They might as well object that the poet has no right to impersonate the dead. We common folk know better. We know that in personating the dear dead, and calling in bell-like tones on the inarticulate living, the poet shall be enabled to break the lightnings of the Beast, and thereby he, being himself, alas! dead, yet speaketh; and shall speak, to ones and twos and a host. As it is written in resonant bronze: VIVOS .VOCO . MORTUOS . PLANGO . FULGURA . FRANGO: words cast by this officer upon a church bell which still rings in far away Orwell in memory of his father — and of mine.

By this time the little room was cold. For some reason the guns had awakened in the Salient. An Indian trooper who had just come up, and did not yet know the orders, blew "Lights out," — on a cavalry trumpet. The sappers work by night. The officer turned and went his way to his accursed trenches, leaving the verse with me.

John McCrae witnessed only once the raw earth of Flanders hide its shame in the warm scarlet glory of the poppy. Others have watched this resurrection of the flowers in four successive seasons, a fresh miracle every time it occurs. Also they have observed the rows of crosses lengthen, the torch thrown, caught, and carried to victory. The dead may sleep. We have not broken faith with them.

It is little wonder then that "In Flanders Fields" has become the poem of the army. The soldiers have learned it with their hearts, which is quite a different thing from committing it to memory. It circulates, as a song should circulate, by the living word of mouth, not by printed characters. That is the true test of poetry, — its insistence on making itself learnt by heart. The army has varied the text; but each variation only serves to reveal more clearly the mind of the maker. The army says, "*Among* the crosses"; "felt dawn *and* sunset glow"; "*Lived* and were loved." The army may be right: it usually is.

Nor has any piece of verse in recent years been more widely known in the civilian world. It was used on every platform from which men were being adjured to adventure their lives or their riches in the great trial through which the present generation has passed. Many "replies" have been made. The best I have seen was written in the *New York Evening Post*. None but those who were prepared to die before Vimy Ridge that early April day of 1916 will ever feel fully the great truth of Mr. Lillard's opening lines, as they speak for all Americans:

> "Rest ye in peace, ye Flanders dead.
> The fight that ye so bravely led
> We've taken up."

They did — and bravely. They heard the cry — "If ye break faith, we shall not sleep."

II
With the Guns

If there was nothing remarkable about the publication of "In Flanders Fields," there was something momentous in the moment of writing it. And yet it was a sure instinct which prompted the writer to send it to *Punch*. A rational man wishes to know the news of the world in which he lives; and if he is interested in life, he is eager to know how men feel and comport themselves amongst the events which are passing. For this purpose *Punch* is the great newspaper of the world, and these lines describe better than any other how men felt in that great moment.

It was in April, 1915. The enemy was in the full cry of victory. All that remained for him was to occupy Paris, as once he did before, and to seize the Channel ports. Then France, England, and the world were doomed. All winter the German had spent in repairing his plans, which had gone somewhat awry on the Marne. He had devised his final stroke, and it fell upon the Canadians at Ypres. This battle, known as the second battle of Ypres, culminated on April 22nd, but it really extended over the whole month.

The inner history of war is written from the recorded impressions of men who have endured it. John McCrae in a series of letters to his mother, cast in the form of a diary, has set down in words the impressions which this event of the war made upon a peculiarly sensitive mind. The account is here transcribed without any attempt at "amplification," or "clarifying" by notes upon incidents or references to places. These are only too well known.

Friday, April 23rd, 1915.

As we moved up last evening, there was heavy firing about 4.30 on our left, the hour at which the general attack with gas was made when the French line broke. We could see the shells bursting over Ypres, and in a small village to our left, meeting General ———, C.R.A., of one of the divisions, he ordered us to halt for orders. We sent forward notifications to our Headquarters, and sent out orderlies to get in touch with the batteries of the farther forward brigades already in action. The story of these guns will be read elsewhere. They had a tough time, but got away safely, and did wonderful service. One battery fired in two opposite directions at once, and both batteries fired at point blank, open sights, at Germans in the open. They were at times quite without infantry on their front, for their position was behind the French to the left of the British line.

As we sat on the road we began to see the French stragglers — men without arms, wounded men, teams, wagons, civilians, refugees — some by the roads, some across country, all talking, shouting — the very picture of débâcle. I must say they were the "tag enders" of a fighting line rather than the line itself. They streamed on, and shouted to us scraps of not too inspiriting information while we stood and took our medicine, and picked out gun positions in the fields in case we had to go in there and then. The men were splendid; not a word; not a shake, and it was a terrific test. Traffic whizzed by — ambulances, transport, ammunition, supplies, despatch riders — and the shells thundered into the town, or burst high in the air nearer us, and the refugees streamed. Women, old men, little children, hopeless, tearful, quiet or excited, tired, dodging the traffic, — and the wounded in singles or in groups. Here and there I could give a momentary help, and the ambulances picked up as they could. So the cold moonlight night wore on — no change save that the towers of Ypres showed up against the glare of the city burning; and the shells still sailed in.

At 9.30 our ammunition column (the part that had been "in") appeared. Major —— had waited, like Casabianca, for orders until the Germans were 500 yards away; then he started, getting safely away save for one wagon lost, and some casualties in men and horses. He found our column, and we prepared to send forward ammunition as soon as we could learn where the batteries had taken up position in retiring, for retire they had to. Eleven, twelve, and finally grey day broke, and we still waited. At 3.45 word came to go in and support a French counterattack at 4.30 A.M. Hastily we got the order spread; it was 4.00 A.M. and three miles to go.

Of one's feelings all this night — of the asphyxiated French soldiers — of the women and children — of the cheery, steady British reinforcements that moved up quietly past us, going up, not back — I could write, but you can imagine.

We took the road at once, and went up at the gallop. The Colonel rode ahead to scout a position (we had only four guns, part of the ammunition column, and the brigade staff; the 1st and 4th batteries were back in reserve at our last billet). Along the roads we went, and made our place on time, pulled up for ten minutes just short of the position, where I put Bonfire [his horse] with my groom in a farmyard, and went forward on foot — only a quarter of a mile or so — then we advanced. Bonfire had soon to move; a shell killed a horse about four yards away from him, and he wisely took other ground. Meantime we went on into the position we were to occupy for seventeen days, though we could not guess that. I can hardly say more than that it was near the Yser Canal.

We got into action at once, under heavy gun-fire. We were to the left entirely of the British line, and behind French troops, and so we remained for eight days. A Colonel of the R.A., known to fame, joined us and camped with us; he was our link with the French Headquarters, and was in local command of the guns in this locality. When he left us eight days later he said, "I am glad to get out of this hell-hole." He was a great comfort to us, for he is very capable, and the entire battle was largely fought "on our own," following the requests of the Infantry on our front, and scarcely guided by our own staff at all. We at once set out to register our targets, and almost at once had to get into steady firing on quite a large sector of front. We dug in the guns as quickly as we could, and took as Headquarters some infantry trenches already sunk on a ridge near the canal. We were subject from the first to a steady and accurate shelling, for we were all but in sight, as were the German trenches about 2000 yards to our front. At times the fire would come in salvos quickly repeated. Bursts of fire would be made for ten or fifteen minutes at a time. We got all varieties of projectile, from 3 inch to 8 inch, or perhaps 10 inch; the small ones usually as air bursts, the larger percussion and air, and the heaviest percussion only.

My work began almost from the start — steady but never overwhelming, except perhaps once for a few minutes. A little cottage behind our ridge served as a cook-house, but was so heavily hit the second day that we had to be chary of it. During bursts of fire I usually took the back slope of the sharply crested ridge for what shelter it offered. At 3 our 1st and 4th arrived, and went into action at once a few hundred yards in our rear. Wires were at once put out, to be cut by shells hundreds and hundreds of times, but always repaired by our indefatigable linemen. So the day wore on; in the night the shelling still kept up: three different German attacks were made and repulsed. If we suffered by being close up, the Germans suffered from us, for already tales of good shooting came down to us. I got some sleep despite the constant firing, for we had none last night.

Saturday, April 24th, 1915.
Behold us now anything less than two miles north of Ypres on the west side of the canal; this runs north, each bank flanked with high elms, with bare trunks of the familiar Netherlands type. A few yards to the West a main road runs, likewise bordered; the Censor will allow me to say that on the high bank between these we had our headquarters; the ridge is perhaps fifteen to twenty feet high, and slopes forward fifty yards to the water, the back is more steep, and slopes

quickly to a little subsidiary water way, deep but dirty. Where the guns were I shall not say; but they were not far, and the German aeroplanes that viewed us daily with all but impunity knew very well. A road crossed over the canal, and interrupted the ridge; across the road from us was our billet — the place we cooked in, at least, and where we usually took our meals. Looking to the south between the trees, we could see the ruins of the city: to the front on the sky line, with rolling ground in the front, pitted by French trenches, the German lines; to the left front, several farms and a windmill, and farther left, again near the canal, thicker trees and more farms. The farms and windmills were soon burnt. Several farms we used for observing posts were also quickly burnt during the next three or four days. All along behind us at varying distances French and British guns; the flashes at night lit up the sky.

These high trees were at once a protection and a danger. Shells that struck them were usually destructive. When we came in the foliage was still very thin. Along the road, which was constantly shelled "on spec" by the Germans, one saw all the sights of war: wounded men limping or carried, ambulances, trains of supply, troops, army mules, and tragedies. I saw one bicycle orderly: a shell exploded and he seemed to pedal on for eight or ten revolutions and then collapsed in a heap — dead. Straggling soldiers would be killed or wounded, horses also, until it got to be a night-mare. I used to shudder every time I saw wagons or troops on that road. My dugout looked out on it. I got a square hole, 8 by 8, dug in the side of the hill (west), roofed over with remnants to keep out the rain, and a little sandbag parapet on the back to prevent pieces of "back-kick shells" from coming in, or prematures from our own or the French guns for that matter. Some straw on the floor completed it. The ground was treacherous and a slip the first night nearly buried ——. So we had to be content with walls straight up and down, and trust to the height of the bank for safety. All places along the bank were more or less alike, all squirrel holes.

This morning we supported a heavy French attack at 4.30; there had been three German attacks in the night, and everyone was tired. We got heavily shelled. In all eight or ten of our trees were cut by shells — cut right off, the upper part of the tree subsiding heavily and straight down, as a usual thing. One would think a piece a foot long was just instantly cut out; and these trees were about 18 inches in diameter. The gas fumes came very heavily: some blew down from the infantry trenches, some came from the shells: one's eyes smarted, and breathing was very laboured. Up to noon to-day we fired 2500 rounds. Last night Col. Morrison and I slept at a French Colonel's headquarters near by, and in the night our room was filled up with wounded. I woke up and shared my bed with a chap with "a wounded leg and a chill." Probably thirty wounded were brought into the one little room.

Col. ——, R.A., kept us in communication with the French General in whose command we were. I bunked down in the trench on the top of the ridge: the sky was red with the glare of the city still burning, and we could hear the almost constant procession of large shells sailing over from our left front into the city: the crashes of their explosion shook the ground where we were. After a terribly hard day, professionally and otherwise, I slept well, but it rained and the trench was awfully muddy and wet.

Sunday, April 25th, 1915.
The weather brightened up, and we got at it again. This day we had several heavy attacks, prefaced by heavy artillery fire; these bursts of fire would result in our getting 100 to 150 rounds right on us or nearby: the heavier our fire (which was on the trenches entirely) the heavier theirs.

Our food supply came up at dusk in wagons, and the water was any we could get, but of course treated with chloride of lime. The ammunition had to be brought down the roads at the gallop, and the more firing the more wagons. The men would quickly carry the rounds to the guns, as the wagons had to halt behind our hill. The good old horses would swing around at the gallop, pull up in an instant, and stand puffing and blowing, but with their heads up, as if to say, "Wasn't that well done?" It makes you want to kiss their dear old noses, and assure them of a peaceful pasture once more. To-day we got our dressing station dugout complete, and slept there at night.

Three farms in succession burned on our front — colour in the otherwise dark. The flashes of shells over the front and rear in all directions. The city still burning and the procession still going on. I dressed a number of French wounded; one Turco prayed to Allah and Mohammed all the time I was dressing his wound. On the front field one can see the dead lying here and there, and in places where an assault has been they lie very thick on the front slopes of the German trenches. Our telephone wagon team hit by a shell; two horses killed and another wounded. I did what I could for the wounded one, and he subsequently got well. This night, beginning after dark, we got a terrible shelling, which kept up till 2 or 3 in the morning. Finally I got to sleep, though it was still going on. We must have got a couple of hundred rounds, in single or pairs. Every one burst over us, would light up the dugout, and every hit in front would shake the ground and bring down small bits of earth on us, or else the earth thrown into the air by the explosion would come spattering down on our roof, and into the front of the dugout. Col. Morrison tried the mess house, but the shelling was too heavy, and he and the adjutant joined Cosgrave and me, and we four spent an anxious night there in the dark. One officer was on watch "on the bridge" (as we called the trench at the top of the ridge) with the telephones.

Monday, April 26th, 1915.
Another day of heavy actions, but last night much French and British artillery has come in, and the place is thick with Germans. There

are many prematures (with so much firing) but the pieces are usually spread before they get to us. It is disquieting, however, I must say. And all the time the birds sing in the trees over our heads. Yesterday up to noon we fired 3000 rounds for the twenty-four hours; to-day we have fired much less, but we have registered fresh fronts, and burned some farms behind the German trenches. About six the fire died down, and we had a peaceful evening and night, and Cosgrave and I in the dugout made good use of it. The Colonel has an individual dugout, and Dodds sleeps "topside" in the trench. To all this, put in a background of anxiety lest the line break, for we are just where it broke before.

Tuesday, April 27th, 1915.

This morning again registering batteries on new points. At 1.30 a heavy attack was prepared by the French and ourselves. The fire was very heavy for half an hour and the enemy got busy too. I had to cross over to the batteries during it, an unpleasant journey. More gas attacks in the afternoon. The French did not appear to press the attack hard, but in the light of subsequent events it probably was only a feint. It seems likely that about this time our people began to thin out the artillery again for use elsewhere; but this did not at once become apparent. At night usually the heavies farther back take up the story, and there is a duel. The Germans fire on our roads after dark to catch reliefs and transport. I suppose ours do the same.

Wednesday, April 28th, 1915.

I have to confess to an excellent sleep last night. At times anxiety says, "I don't want a meal," but experience says "you need your food," so I attend regularly to that. The billet is not too safe either. Much German air reconnaissance over us, and heavy firing from both sides during the day. At 6.45 we again prepared a heavy artillery attack, but the infantry made little attempt to go on. We are perhaps the "chopping block," and our "preparations" may be chiefly designed to prevent detachments of troops being sent from our front elsewhere.

I have said nothing of what goes on on our right and left; but it is equally part and parcel of the whole game; this eight mile front is constantly heavily engaged. At intervals, too, they bombard Ypres. Our back lines, too, have to be constantly shifted on account of shell fire, and we have desultory but constant losses there. In the evening rifle fire gets more frequent, and bullets are constantly singing over us. Some of them are probably ricochets, for we are 1800 yards, or nearly, from the nearest German trench.

Thursday, April 29th, 1915.

This morning our billet was hit. We fire less these days, but still a good deal. There was a heavy French attack on our left. The "gas" attacks can be seen from here. The yellow cloud rising up is for us a signal to open, and we do. The wind is from our side to-day, and a good thing it is. Several days ago during the firing a big Oxford-grey dog, with beautiful brown eyes, came to us in a panic. He ran to me, and pressed his head *hard* against my leg. So I got him a safe place and he sticks by us. We call him Fleabag, for he looks like it.

This night they shelled us again heavily for some hours — the same shorts, hits, overs on percussion, and great yellow-green air bursts. One feels awfully irritated by the constant din — a mixture of anger and apprehension.

Friday, April 30th, 1915.
Thick mist this morning, and relative quietness; but before it cleared the Germans started again to shell us. At 10 it cleared, and from 10 to 2 we fired constantly. The French advanced, and took some ground on our left front and a batch of prisoners. This was at a place we call Twin Farms. Our men looked curiously at the Boches as they were marched through. Some better activity in the afternoon by the Allies' aeroplanes. The German planes have had it too much their way lately. Many of to-day's shells have been very large — 10 or 12 inch; a lot of tremendous holes dug in the fields just behind us.

Saturday, May 1st, 1915.
May day! Heavy bombardment at intervals through the day. Another heavy artillery preparation at 3.25, but no French advance. We fail to understand why, but orders go. We suffered somewhat during the day. Through the evening and night heavy firing at intervals.

Sunday, May 2nd, 1915.

Heavy gunfire again this morning. Lieut. H——
was killed at the guns. His diary's last words were,
"It has quieted a little and I shall try to get a good
sleep." I said the Committal Service over him, as
well as I could from memory. A soldier's death!
Batteries again registering barrages or barriers
of fire at set ranges. At 3 the Germans attacked,
preceded by gas clouds. Fighting went on for an
hour and a half, during which their guns ham-
mered heavily with some loss to us. The French
lines are very uneasy, and we are correspondingly
anxious. The infantry fire was very heavy, and
we fired incessantly, keeping on into the night.
Despite the heavy fire I got asleep at 12, and slept
until daylight which comes at 3.

Monday, May 3rd, 1915.

A clear morning, and the accursed German aero-
planes over our positions again. They are usually
fired at, but no luck. To-day a shell on our hill
dug out a cannon ball about six inches in diame-
ter — probably of Napoleon's or earlier times —
heavily rusted. A German attack began, but half
an hour of artillery fire drove it back. Major——,
R.A., was up forward, and could see the German
reserves. Our 4th was turned on: first round 100
over; shortened and went into gunfire, and his
report was that the effect was perfect. The same
occurred again in the evening, and again at mid-
night. The Germans were reported to be con-
stantly massing for attack, and we as constantly
"went to them." The German guns shelled us as
usual at intervals. This must get very tiresome to

read; but through it all, it must be mentioned that the constantly broken communications have to be mended, rations and ammunition brought up, the wounded to be dressed and got away. Our dugouts have the French Engineers and French Infantry next door by turns. They march in and out. The back of the hill is a network of wires, so that one has to go carefully.

Tuesday, May 4th, 1915.

Despite intermittent shelling and some casualties the quietest day yet; but we live in an uneasy atmosphere as German attacks are constantly being projected, and our communications are interrupted and scrappy. We get no news of any sort and have just to sit tight and hold on. Evening closed in rainy and dark. Our dugout is very slenderly provided against it, and we get pretty wet and very dirty. In the quieter morning hours we get a chance of a wash and occasionally a shave.

Wednesday, May 5th, 1915.

Heavily hammered in the morning from 7 to 9, but at 9 it let up; the sun came out and things looked better. Evidently our line has again been thinned of artillery and the requisite minimum to hold is left. There were German attacks to our right, just out of our area. Later on we and they both fired heavily, the first battery getting it especially hot. The planes over us again and again, to coach the guns. An attack expected at dusk, but it turned only to heavy night shelling, so that with our fire, theirs, and the infantry cracking away constantly, we got sleep in small quantity all night; bullets whizzing over us constantly. Heavy rain from 5 to 8, and everything wet except the far-in corner of the dugout, where we mass our things to keep them as dry as we may.

Thursday, May 6th, 1915.
After the rain a bright morning; the leaves and blossoms are coming out. We ascribe our quietude to a welcome flock of allied planes which are over this morning. The Germans attacked at eleven, and again at six in the afternoon, each meaning a waking up of heavy artillery on the whole front. In the evening we had a little rain at intervals, but it was light.

Friday, May 7th, 1915.
A bright morning early, but clouded over later. The Germans gave it to us very heavily. There was heavy fighting to the south-east of us. Two attacks or threats, and we went in again.

Saturday, May 8th, 1915.
For the last three days we have been under British divisional control, and supporting our own men who have been put farther to the left, till they are almost in front of us. It is an added comfort. We have four officers out with various infantry regiments for observation and co-operation; they have to stick it in trenches, as all the houses and barns are burned. The whole front is constantly ablaze with big gunfire; the racket never ceases. We have now to do most of the work for our left, as our line appears to be much thinner than it was. A German attack followed the shelling at

7; we were fighting hard till 12, and less regularly all the afternoon. We suffered much, and at one time were down to seven guns. Of these two were smoking at every joint, and the levers were so hot that the gunners used sacking for their hands. The pace is now much hotter, and the needs of the infantry for fire more insistent. The guns are in bad shape by reason of dirt, injuries, and heat. The wind fortunately blows from us, so there is no gas, but the attacks are still very heavy. Evening brought a little quiet, but very disquieting news (which afterwards proved untrue); and we had to face a possible retirement. You may imagine our state of mind, unable to get anything sure in the uncertainty, except that we should stick out as long as the guns would fire, and we could fire them. That sort of night brings a man down to his "bare skin," I promise you. The night was very cold, and not a cheerful one.

Sunday, May 9th, 1915.

At 4 we were ordered to get ready to move, and the Adjutant picked out new retirement positions; but a little later better news came, and the daylight and sun revived us a bit. As I sat in my dugout a little white and black dog with tan spots bolted in over the parapet, during heavy firing, and going to the farthest corner began to dig furiously. Having scraped out a pathetic little hole two inches deep, she sat down and shook, looking most plaintively at me. A few minutes later, her owner came along, a French soldier. Bissac was her name, but she would not leave me at the time. When I sat down a little later, she stole out and shyly crawled in between me and the wall; she stayed by me all day, and I hope got later on to safe quarters.

Firing kept up all day. In thirty hours we had fired 3600 rounds, and at times with seven, eight, or nine guns; our wire cut and repaired eighteen times. Orders came to move, and we got ready. At dusk we got the guns out by hand, and all batteries assembled at a given spot in comparative safety. We were much afraid they would open on us, for at 10 o'clock they gave us 100 or 150 rounds, hitting the trench parapet again and again. However, we were up the road, the last wagon half a mile away before they opened. One burst near me, and splattered some pieces around, but we got clear, and by 12 were out of the usual fire zone. Marched all night, tired as could be, but happy to be clear.

I was glad to get on dear old Bonfire again. We made about sixteen miles, and got to our billets at dawn. I had three or four hours' sleep, and arose to a peaceful breakfast. We shall go back to the line elsewhere very soon, but it is a present relief, and the next place is sure to be better, for it cannot be worse. Much of this narrative is bald and plain, but it tells our part in a really great battle. I have only had hasty notes to go by; in conversation there is much one could say that would be of greater interest. Heard of the *Lusitania* disaster on our road out. A terrible affair!

Here ends the account of his part in this memorable battle, and here follow some general observations upon the experience:

NORTHERN FRANCE, May 10th, 1915.

We got here to refit and rest this morning at

4, having marched last night at 10. The general impression in my mind is of a nightmare. We have been in the most bitter of fights. For seventeen days and seventeen nights none of us have had our clothes off, nor our boots even, except occasionally. In all that time while I was awake, gunfire and rifle fire never ceased for sixty seconds, and it was sticking to our utmost by a weak line all but ready to break, knowing nothing of what was going on, and depressed by reports of anxious infantry. The men and the divisions are worthy of all praise that can be given. It did not end in four days when many of our infantry were taken out. It kept on at fever heat till yesterday.

This, of course, is the second battle of Ypres, or the battle of the Yser, I do not know which. At one time we were down to seven guns, but those guns were smoking at every joint, the gunners using cloth to handle the breech levers because of the heat. We had three batteries in action with four guns added from the other units. Our casualties were half the number of men in the firing line. The horse lines and the wagon lines farther back suffered less, but the Brigade list has gone far higher than any artillery normal. I know one brigade R.A. that was in the Mons retreat and had about the same. I have done what fell to hand. My clothes, boots, kit, and dugout at various times were sadly bloody. Two of our batteries are reduced to two officers each. We have had constant accurate shell-fire, but we have given back no less. And behind it all was the constant background of the sights of the dead, the wounded, the maimed, and a terrible anxiety lest the line should give way.

During all this time, we have been behind French troops, and only helping our own people by oblique fire when necessary. Our horses have suffered heavily too. Bonfire had a light wound from a piece of shell; it is healing and the dear old fellow is very fit. Had my first ride for seventeen days last night. We never saw horses but with the wagons bringing up the ammunition. When fire was hottest they had to come two miles on a road terribly swept, and they did it magnificently. But how tired we are! Weary in body and wearier in mind. None of our men went off their heads but men in units nearby did — and no wonder.

FRANCE, May 12th, 1915.
I am glad you had your mind at rest by the rumour that we were in reserve. What newspaper work! The poor old artillery never gets any mention, and the whole show is the infantry. It may interest you to note on your map a spot on the west bank of the canal, a mile and a half north of Ypres, as the scene of our labours. There can be no harm in saying so, now that we are out of it. The unit was the most advanced of all the Allies' guns by a good deal except one French battery which stayed in a position yet more advanced for two days, and then had to be taken out. I think it may be said that we saw the show from the soup to the coffee.

FRANCE, May 17th, 1915.
The farther we get away from Ypres the more we learn of the enormous power the Germans put in to push us over. Lord only knows how

many men they had, and how many they lost.
I wish I could embody on paper some of the
varied sensations of that seventeen days. All the
gunners down this way passed us all sorts of
"*kudos*" over it. Our guns — those behind us,
from which we had to dodge occasional pre-
matures — have a peculiar bang-sound added
to the sharp crack of discharge. The French 75
has a sharp wood-block-chop sound, and the
shell goes over with a peculiar whine — not
unlike a cat, but beginning with n — thus, —
n-eouw. The big fellows, 3000 yards or more
behind, sounded exactly like our own, but the
flash came three or four seconds before the
sound. Of the German shells — the field guns
come with a great velocity — no warning —
just whizz-bang; white smoke, nearly always air
bursts. The next size, probably 5 inch howitzers,
have a perceptible time of approach, an increas-
ing whine, and a great burst on the percussion
— dirt in all directions. And even if a shell hit
on the front of the canal bank, and one were on
the back of the bank, five, eight, or ten seconds
later one would hear a belated *whirr*, and curved
pieces of shell would light — probably para-
bolic curves or boomerangs. These shells have
a great back kick; from the field gun shrapnel
we got nothing *behind* the shell — all the pieces
go forward. From the howitzers, the danger is
almost as great behind as in front if they burst
on percussion. Then the large shrapnel — air-
burst — have a double explosion, as if a giant
shook a wet sail for two flaps; first a dark green
burst of smoke; then a lighter yellow burst goes

out from the centre, forwards. I do not understand the why of it.

Then the 10-inch shells: a deliberate whirring course — a deafening explosion — black smoke, and earth 70 or 80 feet in the air. These always burst on percussion. The constant noise of our own guns is really worse on the nerves than the shell; there is the deafening noise, and the constant whirr of shells going overhead. The earth shakes with every nearby gun and every close shell. I think I may safely enclose a cross section of our position. The left is the front: a slope down of 20 feet in 100 yards to the canal, a high row of trees on each bank, then a short 40 yards slope up to the summit of the trench, where the brain of the outfit was; then a telephone wired slope, and on the sharp slope, the dugouts, including my own. The nondescript affair on the low slope is the gun position, behind it the men's shelter pits. Behind my dugout was a rapid small stream, on its far bank a row of pollard willows, then 30 yards of field, then a road with two parallel rows of high trees. Behind this again, several hundred yards of fields to cross before the main gun positions are reached.

More often fire came from three quarters left, and because our ridge died away there was a low spot over which they could come pretty dangerously. The road thirty yards behind us was a nightmare to me. I saw all the tragedies of war enacted there. A wagon, or a bunch of horses, or a stray man, or a couple of men, would get there just in time for a shell. One would see the absolute knock-out, and the obviously lightly wounded crawling off on hands and knees; or worse yet, at night, one would hear the tragedy — "that horse scream" — or the man's moan. All our own wagons had to come there (one every half hour in smart action), be emptied, and the ammunition carried over by hand. Do you wonder that the road got on our nerves? On this road, too, was the house where we took our meals. It was hit several times, windows all blown in by nearby shells, but one end remained for us.

Seventeen days of Hades! At the end of the first day if anyone had told us we had to spend seventeen days there, we would have folded our

Looking S. from our position. The 'back slope' in the foreground.

Facsimile of a sketch by John McCrae on the back of a card.

hands and said it could not be done. On the fifteenth day we got orders to go out, but that was countermanded in two hours. To the last we could scarcely believe we were actually to get out. The real audacity of the position was its safety; the Germans knew to a foot where we were. I think I told you of some of the "you must stick it out" messages we got from our [French] General, — they put it up to us. It is a wonder to me that we slept when, and how, we did. If we had not slept and eaten as well as possible we could not have lasted. And while we were doing this, the London office of a Canadian newspaper cabled home "Canadian Artillery in reserve." Such is fame!

Thursday, May 27th, 1915.
Day cloudy and chilly. We wore our greatcoats most of the afternoon, and looked for bits of sunlight to get warm. About two o'clock the heavy guns gave us a regular "black-smithing." Every time we fired we drew a perfect hornet's nest about our heads. While attending to a casualty, a shell broke through both sides of the trench, front and back, about twelve feet away. The zigzag of the trench was between it and us, and we escaped. From my bunk the moon looks down at me, and the wind whistles along the trench like a corridor. As the trenches run in all directions they catch the wind however it blows, so one is always sure of a good draught. We have not had our clothes off since last Saturday, and there is no near prospect of getting them off.

Friday, May 28th, 1915.

Warmer this morning and sunny, a quiet morn-
ing, as far as we were concerned. One battery
fired twenty rounds and the rest "sat tight."
Newspapers which arrive show that up to May
7th, the Canadian public has made no guess at
the extent of the battle of Ypres. The Canadian
papers seem to have lost interest in it after the
first four days; this regardless of the fact that the
artillery, numerically a quarter of the division,
was in all the time. One correspondent writes
from the Canadian rest camp, and never mentions
Ypres. Others say they hear heavy bombarding
which appears to come from Armentires.

A few strokes will complete the picture:

Wednesday, April 29th, 1915.

This morning is the sixth day of this fight; it has
been constant, except that we got good chance
to sleep for the last two nights. Our men have
fought beyond praise. Canadian soldiers have set a
standard for themselves which will keep posterity
busy to surpass. And the War Office published that
the 4.1 guns captured were Canadian. They were
not: the division has not lost a gun so far by cap-
ture. We will make a good job of it — if we can.

May 1st, 1915.

This is the ninth day that we have stuck to
the ridge, and the batteries have fought with a
steadiness which is beyond all praise. If I could
say what our casualties in men, guns, and horses
were, you would see at a glance it has been a

hot corner; but we have given better than we got, for the German casualties from this front have been largely from artillery, except for the French attack of yesterday and the day before, when they advanced appreciably on our left. The front, however, just here remains where it was, and the artillery fire is very heavy — I think as heavy here as on any part of the line, with the exception of certain cross-roads which are the particular object of fire. The first four days the anxiety was wearing, for we did not know at what minute the German army corps would come for us. We lie out in support of the French troops entirely, and are working with them. Since that time evidently great reinforcements have come in, and now we have a most formidable force of artillery to turn on them.

Fortunately the weather has been good; the days are hot and summerlike. Yesterday in the press of bad smells I got a whiff of a hedgerow in bloom. The birds perch on the trees over our heads and twitter away as if there was nothing to worry about. Bonfire is still well. I do hope he gets through all right.

FLANDERS, March 30th, 1915.

The Brigade is actually in twelve different places. The ammunition column and the horse and wagon lines are back, and my corporal visits them every day. I attend the gun lines; any casualty is reported by telephone, and I go to it. The wounded and sick stay where they are till dark, when the field ambulances go over certain grounds and collect. A good deal of suffering is entailed by the delay till night, but it is useless for vehicles to go on the roads within 1500 yards of the trenches. They are willing enough to go. Most of the trench injuries are of the head, and therefore there is a high proportion of killed in the daily warfare as opposed to an attack. Our Canadian plots fill up rapidly.

And here is one last note to his mother:

On the eve of the battle of Ypres I was indebted to you for a letter which said "take good care of my son Jack, but I would not have you unmindful that, sometimes, when we save we lose." I have that last happy phrase to thank. Often when I had to go out over the areas that were being shelled, it came into my mind. I would shoulder the box, and "go to it."

At this time the Canadian division was moving south to take its share in the events that happened in the La Bassée sector. Here is the record:

Tuesday, June 1st, 1915.
1½ miles northeast of Festubert, near La Bassée. Last night a 15 pr. and a 4-inch howitzer fired at intervals of five minutes from 8 till 4; most of them within 500 or 600 yards — a very tiresome procedure; much of it is on registered roads. In the morning I walked out to Le Touret to the wagon lines, got Bonfire, and rode to the head-quarters at Vendin-lez-Bethune, a little village a mile past Bethune. Left the horse at the lines and walked back again. An unfortunate shell in the 1st

killed a sergeant and wounded two men; thanks to the strong emplacements the rest of the crew escaped. In the evening went around the batteries and said good-bye. We stood by while they laid away the sergeant who was killed. Kind hands have made two pathetic little wreaths of roses; the grave under an apple-tree, and the moon rising over the horizon; a siege-lamp held for the book. Of the last 41 days the guns have been in action 33. Captain Lockhart, late with Fort Garry Horse, arrived to relieve me. I handed over, came up to the horse lines, and slept in a covered wagon in a courtyard. We were all sorry to part — the four of us have been very intimate and had agreed perfectly — and friendships under these circumstances are apt to be the real thing. I am sorry to leave them in such a hot corner, but cannot choose and must obey orders. It is a great relief from strain, I must admit, to be out, but I could wish that they all were.

This phase of the war lasted two months precisely, and to John McCrae it must have seemed a lifetime since he went into this memorable action. The events preceding the second battle of Ypres received scant mention in his letters; but one remains, which brings into relief one of the many moves of that tumultuous time.

April 1st, 1915.
We moved out in the late afternoon, getting on the road a little after dark. Such a move is not unattended by danger, for to bring horses and limbers down the roads in the shell zone in daylight renders them liable to observation, aerial

or otherwise. More than that, the roads are now beginning to be dusty, and at all times there is the noise which carries far. The roads are nearly all registered in their battery books, so if they suspect a move, it is the natural thing to loose off a few rounds. However, our anxiety was not borne out, and we got out of the danger zone by 8.30 — a not too long march in the dark, and then for the last of the march a glorious full moon. The houses everywhere are as dark as possible, and on the roads noises but no lights. One goes on by the long rows of trees that are so numerous in this country, on cobblestones and country roads, watching one's horses' ears wagging, and seeing not much else. Our maps are well studied before we start, and this time we are not far out of familiar territory. We got to our new billet about 10 — quite a good farmhouse; and almost at once one feels the relief of the strain of being in the shell zone. I cannot say I had noticed it when there; but one is distinctly relieved when out of it.

Such, then, was the life in Flanders fields in which the verse was born. This is no mere surmise. There is a letter from Major-General E.W.B. Morrison, C.B., C.M.G., D.S.O., who commanded the Brigade at the time, which is quite explicit. "This poem," General Morrison writes, "was literally born of fire and blood during the hottest phase of the second battle of Ypres. My headquarters were in a trench on the top of the bank of the Ypres Canal, and John had his dressing station in a hole dug in the foot of the bank. During periods in the battle men who were shot actually rolled down the bank into his dressing station. Along from us a few hundred yards was the headquarters of a regiment, and many times during the sixteen days of battle, he and I watched them burying their dead whenever there was a lull. Thus the crosses, row on row, grew into a good-sized cemetery. Just as he describes, we often heard in the mornings the larks singing high in the air, between the crash of the shell and the reports of the guns in the battery just beside us. I have a letter from him in which he mentions having written the poem to pass away the time between the arrival of batches of wounded, and partly as an experiment with several varieties of poetic metre. I have a sketch of the scene, taken at the time, including his dressing station; and during our operations at Passchendaele last November, I found time to make a sketch of the scene of the crosses, row on row, from which he derived his inspiration."

The last letter from the Front is dated June 1st, 1915. Upon that day he was posted to No. 3 General Hospital at Boulogne, and placed in charge of medicine with the rank of Lieutenant-Colonel as of date 17th April, 1915. Here he remained until the day of his death on January 28th, 1918.

III
The Brand of War

There are men who pass through such scenes unmoved. If they have eyes, they do not see; and ears, they do not hear. But John McCrae was profoundly moved, and bore in his body until the end the signs of his experience. Before taking up his new duties he made a visit to the hospitals in Paris to see if there was any new thing that might be learned. A Nursing Sister in the American Ambulance at Neuilly-sur-Seine met him in the wards. Although she had known him for fifteen years she did not recognize him, — he appeared to her so old, so worn, his face lined and ashen grey in colour, his expression dull, his action slow and heavy.

To those who have never seen John McCrae since he left Canada this change in his appearance will seem incredible. He was of the Eckfords, and the Eckford men were "bonnie men," men with rosy cheeks. It was a year before I met him again, and he had not yet recovered from the strain. Although he was upwards of forty years of age when he left Canada he had always retained an appearance of extreme youthfulness. He frequented the company of men much younger than himself, and their youth was imputed to him. His frame was tall and well knit, and he showed alertness in every move. He would arise from the chair with every muscle in action, and walk forth as if he were about to dance.

The first time I saw him he was doing an autopsy at the Montreal General Hospital upon the body of a child who had died under my care. This must have been in the year 1900, and the impression of boyishness remained until I met him in France sixteen years later. His manner of dress did much to produce this illusion. When he was a student in London he employed a tailor in Queen Victoria Street to make his clothes; but with advancing years he neglected to have new measurements taken or to alter the pattern of his cloth. To obtain a new suit was merely to write a letter, and he was always economical of time. In those days jackets were cut short, and he adhered to the fashion with persistent care.

This appearance of youth at times caused chagrin to those patients who had heard of his fame as a physician, and called upon him for the first time. In the Royal Victoria Hospital, after he had been appointed physician, he entered the wards and asked a nurse to fetch a screen so that he might examine a patient in privacy.

"Students are not allowed to use screens," the young woman warned him with some asperity in her voice.

If I were asked to state briefly the impression which remains with me most firmly, I should say it was one of continuous laughter. That is not true, of course, for in repose his face was heavy, his countenance more than ruddy; it was even of a "choleric" cast, and at times almost livid, especially when he was recovering from one of those attacks of asthma from which he habitually suffered. But his smile was his own, and it was ineffable. It filled the eyes, and illumined the face. It was the smile of sheer fun, of pure gaiety, of sincere playfulness, innocent of irony; with a tinge of sarcasm — never. When he allowed himself to speak of meanness in the profession, of dishonesty in men, of evil in the world, his face became formidable. The glow of his countenance deepened; his words were bitter, and the tones harsh. But the indignation would not last. The smile would come back. The effect was spoiled. Everyone laughed with him.

After his experience at the front the old gaiety never returned. There were moments of irascibility and moods of irritation. The desire for solitude grew upon him, and with Bonfire and Bonneau he would go apart for long afternoons far afield by the roads and lanes about Boulogne. The truth is: he felt that he and all had failed, and that the torch was thrown from failing hands. We have heard much of the suffering, the misery, the cold, the wet, the gloom of those first three winters; but no tongue has yet uttered the inner misery of heart that was bred of those three years of failure to break the enemy's force.

He was not alone in this shadow of deep darkness. Givenchy, Festubert, Neuve-Chapelle, Ypres, Hooge, the Somme — to mention alone the battles in which up to that time the Canadian Corps had been engaged — all ended in failure; and to a sensitive and foreboding mind there were sounds and signs that it would be given to this generation to hear the pillars and fabric of Empire come crashing into the abysm of chaos. He was not at the Somme in that October of 1916, but those who returned up north with the remnants of their division from that place of slaughter will remember that, having done all men could do, they felt like deserters because they had not left their poor bodies dead upon the field along with friends of a lifetime, comrades of a campaign. This is no mere matter of surmise. The last day I spent with him we talked of those things in his tent, and I testify that it is true.

IV
Going to the Wars

John McCrae went to the war without illusions. At first, like many others of his age, he did not "think of enlisting," although "his services are at the disposal of the Country if it needs them."

In July, 1914, he was at work upon the second edition of the *Text-Book of Pathology* by Adami and McCrae, published by Messrs. Lea and Febiger, and he had gone to Philadelphia to read the proofs. He took them to Atlantic City where he could "sit out on the sand, and get sunshine and oxygen, and work all at once."

It was a laborious task, passing eighty to a hundred pages of highly technical print each day. Then there was the index, between six and seven thousand items. "I have," so he writes, "to change every item in the old index and add others. I have a pile of pages, 826 in all. I look at the index, find the old page among the 826, and then change the number. This about 7000 times, so you may guess the drudgery." On July 15th, the work was finished, registered, and entrusted to the mail with a special delivery stamp. The next day he wrote the preface, "which really finished the job." In very truth his scientific work was done.

It was now midsummer. The weather was hot. He returned to Montreal. Practice was dull. He was considering a voyage to Havre and "a little trip with Dr. Adami" when he arrived. On July 29th, he left Canada "for better or worse. With the world so disturbed," he records, "I would gladly have stayed more in touch with events, but I dare say one is just as happy away from the hundred conflicting reports." The ship was the *Scotian* of the Allan Line, and he "shared a comfortable cabin with a professor of Greek," who was at the University in his own time.

For one inland born, he had a keen curiosity about ships and the sea. There is a letter written when he was thirteen years of age in which he gives an account of a visit to a naval exhibition in London. He describes the models which he saw, and gives an elaborate table of names, dimensions, and tonnage. He could identify the house flags and funnels of all the principal liners; he could follow a ship through all her vicissitudes and change of ownership. When he found himself in a seaport town his first business was to visit the water front and take knowledge of the vessels that lay in the stream or by the docks. One voyage he made to England was in a cargo ship. With his passion for work he took on the duties of surgeon, and amazed the skipper with a revelation of the new technique in operations which he himself had been accustomed to perform by the light of experience alone.

On the present and more luxurious voyage, he remarks that the decks were roomy, the ship seven years old, and capable of fifteen knots an hour, the passengers pleasant, and including a large number of French. All now know only too well the nature of the business which sent those ardent spirits flocking home to their native land.

Forty-eight hours were lost in fog. The weather was too thick for making the Straits, and the *Scotian* proceeded by Cape Race on her way to Havre. Under date of August 5–6 the first reference to the war appears: "All is excitement; the ship runs without lights. Surely the German kaiser has his head in the noose at last: it will be a terrible war, and the finish of one or the other. I am afraid my holiday trip is knocked galley west; but we shall see." The voyage continues. A "hundred miles from Moville we turned back, and headed South for Queenstown; thence to the Channel; put in at Portland; a squadron of battleships; arrived here this morning."

The problem presented itself to him as to many another. The decision was made. To go back to America was to go back from the war. Here are the words: "It seems quite impossible to return, and I do not think I should try. I would not feel quite comfortable over it. I am cabling to Morrison at Ottawa, that I am available either as combatant or medical if they need me. I do not go to it very light-heartedly, but I think it is up to me."

It was not so easy in those days to get to the war, as he and many others were soon to discover. There was in Canada at the time a small permanent force of 3000 men, a military college, a Headquarters staff, and divisional staff for the various districts into which the country was divided. In addition there was a body of militia with a strength of about 60,000 officers and other ranks. Annual camps were formed at which all arms of the service were represented, and the whole was a very good imitation of service conditions. Complete plans for mobilization were in existence, by which a certain quota, according to the establishment required, could be detailed from each district. But upon the outbreak of war the operations were taken in hand by a Minister of Militia who assumed in his own person all those duties usually assigned to the staff. He called to his assistance certain business and political associates, with the result that volunteers who followed military methods did not get very far.

Accordingly we find it written in John McCrae's diary from London: "Nothing doing here. I have yet no word from the Department at Ottawa, but I try to be philosophical until I hear from Morrison. If they want me for the Canadian forces, I could use my old Sam Browne belt, sword, and saddle if it is yet extant. At times I wish I could go home with a clear conscience."

He sailed for Canada in the *Calgarian* on August 28th, having received a cablegram from Colonel Morrison, that he had been provisionally appointed surgeon to the 1st Brigade Artillery. The night he arrived in Montreal I dined with him at the University Club, and he was aglow with enthusiasm over this new adventure. He remained in Montreal for a few days, and on September 9th, joined the unit to which he was attached as medical officer. Before leaving Montreal he wrote to his sister Geills:

"Out on the awful old trail again! And with very mixed feelings, but some determination. I am off to Val-cartier to-night. I was really afraid to go home, for I feared it would only be harrowing for Mater, and I think she agrees. We can hope for happier times. Everyone most kind and helpful: my going does not seem to surprise anyone. I know you will understand it is hard to go home, and perhaps easier for us all that I do not. I am in good hope of coming back soon and safely: that, I am glad to say, is in other and better hands than ours."

V
South Africa

In the Autumn of 1914, after John McCrae had gone over-seas, I was in a warehouse in Montreal, in which one might find an old piece of mahogany wood. His boxes were there in storage, with his name plainly printed upon them. The storeman, observing my interest, remarked: "This Doctor McCrae cannot be doing much business; he is always going to the wars." The remark was profoundly significant of the state of mind upon the subject of war which prevailed at the time in Canada in more intelligent persons. To this storeman war merely meant that the less usefully employed members of the community sent their boxes to him for safe-keeping until their return. War was a great holiday from work; and he had a vague remembrance that some fifteen years before this customer had required of him a similar service when the South African war broke out.

Either *in esse* or *in posse* John McCrae had "always been going to the wars." At fourteen years of age he joined the Guelph Highland Cadets, and rose to the rank of 1st Lieutenant. As his size and strength increased he reverted to the ranks and transferred to the Artillery. In due time he rose from gunner to major. The formal date of his "Gazette" is 17–3–02 as they write it in the army; but he earned his rank in South Africa.

War was the burden of his thought; war and death the theme of his verse. At the age of thirteen we find him at a gallery in Nottingham, writing this note: "I saw the picture of the artillery going over the trenches at Tel-el-Kebir. It is a good picture; but there are four teams on the guns. Perhaps an extra one had to be put on." If his nomenclature was not correct, the observation of the young artillerist was exact. Such excesses were not permitted in his father's battery in Guelph, Ontario. During this same visit his curiosity led him into the House of Lords, and the sum of his written observation is, "When someone is speaking no one seems to listen at all."

His mother I never knew. Canada is a large place. With his father I had four hours' talk from seven to eleven one June evening in London in 1917. At the time I was on leave from France to give the Cavendish Lecture, a task which demanded some thought; and after two years in the army it was a curious sensation — watching one's mind at work again. The day was Sunday. I had walked down to the river to watch the flowing tide. To one brought up in a country of streams and a moving sea the curse of Flanders is her stagnant waters. It is little wonder the exiles from the Judæan hillsides wept beside the slimy River.

The Thames by evening in June, memories that reached from Tacitus to Wordsworth, the embrasure that extends in front of the Egyptian obelisk for a standing place, and some children "swimming a dog"; — that was the scene and circumstance of my first meeting with his father. A man of middle age was standing by. He wore the flashings of a Lieutenant-Colonel and for badges the Artillery grenades. He seemed a friendly man; and under the influence of the moment, which he also surely felt, I spoke to him.

"A fine river," — That was a safe remark.

"But I know a finer."

"Pharpar and Abana?" I put the stranger to the test.

"No," he said. "The St. Lawrence is not of Damascus." He had answered to the sign, and looked at my patches.

"I have a son in France, myself," he said. "His name is McCrae."

"Not John McCrae?"

"John McCrae is my son."

The resemblance was instant, but this was an older man than at first sight he seemed to be. I asked him to dinner at Morley's, my place of resort for a length of time beyond the memory of all but the oldest servants. He had already dined but he came and sat with me, and told me marvellous things.

David McCrae had raised, and trained, a field battery in Guelph, and brought it overseas. He was at the time upwards of seventy years of age, and was considered on account of years alone "unfit" to proceed to the front. For many years he had commanded a field battery in the Canadian militia, went on manoeuvres with his "cannons," and fired round shot. When the time came for using shells he bored the fuse with a gimlet; and if the gimlet were lost in the grass, the gun was out of action until the useful tool could be found. This "cannon ball" would travel over the country according to the obstacles it encountered and, "if it struck a man, it might break his leg."

In such a martial atmosphere the boy was brought up, and he was early nourished with the history of the Highland regiments. Also from his father he inherited, or had instilled into him, a love of the out of doors, a knowledge of trees, and plants, a sympathy with birds and beasts, domestic and wild. When the South African war broke out a contingent was dispatched from Canada, but it was so small that few of those desiring to go could find a place. This explains the genesis of the following letter:

I see by to-night's bulletin that there is to be no second contingent. I feel sick with disappointment, and do not believe that I have ever been so disappointed in my life, for ever since this business began I am certain there have not been fifteen minutes of my waking hours that it has not been in my mind. It has to come sooner or later. One campaign might cure me, but nothing else ever will, unless it should be old age. I regret bitterly that I did not enlist with the first, for I doubt if ever another chance will offer like it. This is not said in ignorance of what the hardships would be.

I am ashamed to say I am doing my work in a merely mechanical way. If they are taking surgeons on the other side, I have enough money to get myself across. If I knew any one over there who could do anything, I would certainly set about it. If I can get an appointment in England by going, I will go. My position here I do not count as an old boot in comparison.

In the end he accomplished the desire of his heart, and sailed on the *Laurentian*. Concerning the voyage one transcription will be enough:

On orderly duty. I have just been out taking the picket at 11.30 P.M. In the stables the long row of heads in the half-darkness, the creaking of the ship, the shivering of the hull from the vibration of the engines, the sing of a sentry on the spar deck to some passer-by. Then to the forward deck: the sky half covered with scudding clouds, the stars bright in the intervals, the wind whistling a regular blow that tries one's ears, the constant swish as she settles down to a sea; and, looking aft, the funnel with a wreath of smoke trailing away off into the darkness on the starboard quarter; the patch of white on the funnel discernible dimly; the masts drawing maps across the sky as one looks up; the clank of shovels coming up through the ventilators, — if you have ever been there, you know it all.

There was a voluntary service at six; two ships' lanterns and the men all around, the background of sky and sea, and the strains of "Nearer my God to Thee" rising up in splendid chorus. It was a very effective scene, and it occurred to me that *this* was "the rooibaatjees singing on the road," as the song says.

The next entry is from South Africa:

GREEN POINT CAMP, CAPETOWN,
February 25th, 1900.
You have no idea of the *work*. Section command-
ers live with their sections, which is the right way.
It makes long hours. I never knew a softer bed
than the ground is these nights. I really enjoy
every minute though there is anxiety. We have
lost all our spare horses. We have only enough to
turn out the battery and no more.

After a description of a number of the regiments camped near
by them, he speaks of the Indian troops, and then says:

*John McCrae with fellow officers in South Africa. He is second from left in the
middle row wearing his wedge cap.*

We met the High Priest of it all, and I had a five minutes' chat with him—Kipling I mean. He visited the camp. He looks like his pictures, and is very affable. He told me I spoke like a Winnipeger. He said we ought to "fine the men for drinking unboiled water. Don't give them C.B.; it is no good. Fine them, or drive common sense into them. All Canadians have common sense."

The next letter is from the Lines of Communication:

VAN WYKS VLEI,
March 22nd, 1900.
Here I am with my first command. Each place we strike is a little more God-forsaken than the last, and this place wins up to date. We marched last week from Victoria west to Carnovan, about 80 miles. We stayed there over Sunday, and on Monday my section was detached with mounted infantry, I being the only artillery officer. We marched 54 miles in 37 hours with stops; not very fast, but quite satisfactory. My horse is doing well, although very thin. Night before last on the road we halted, and I dismounted for a minute. When we started I pulled on the lines but no answer. The poor old chap was fast asleep in his tracks, and in about thirty seconds too.

This continuous marching is really hard work. The men at every halt just drop down in the road and sleep until they are kicked up again in ten minutes. They do it willingly too. I am commanding officer, adjutant, officer on duty, and all the rest since we left the main body. Talk about the Army in Flanders! You should hear this battalion. I always knew soldiers could swear, but you ought to hear these fellows. I am told the first contingent has got a name among the regulars.

Three weeks later he writes:

April 10th, 1900.
We certainly shall have done a good march when we get to the railroad, 478 miles through a country desolate of forage carrying our own transport and one-half rations of forage, and frequently the men's rations. For two days running we had nine hours in the saddle without food. My throat was sore and swollen for a day or two, and I felt so sorry for myself at times that I laughed to think how I must have looked: sitting on a stone, drinking a pan of tea without trimmings, that had got cold, and eating a shapeless lump of brown bread; my one "hank" drawn around my neck, serving as hank and bandage alternately. It is miserable to have to climb up on one's horse with a head like a buzz saw, the sun very hot, and "gargle" in one's water bottle. It is surprising how I can go without water if I have to on a short stretch, that is, of ten hours in the sun. It is after nightfall that the thirst really seems to attack one and actually gnaws. One thinks of all the cool drinks and good things one would like to eat. Please understand that this is not for one instant in any spirit of growling.

The detail was now established at Victoria Road. Three entries appear:

April 23rd, 1900.

We are still here in camp hoping for orders to move, but they have not yet come. Most of the other troops have gone. A squadron of the M.C.R., my messmates for the past five weeks, have gone and I am left an orphan. I was very sorry to see them go. They, in the kindness of their hearts, say, if I get stranded, they will do the best they can to get a troop for me in the squadron or some such employment. Impracticable, but kind. I have no wish to cease to be a gunner.

VICTORIA ROAD, May 20th, 1900.

The horses are doing as well as one can expect, for the rations are insufficient. Our men have been helping to get ready a rest camp near us, and have been filling mattresses with hay. Every fatigue party comes back from the hospital, their jackets bulging with hay for the horses. Two bales were condemned as too musty to put into the mattresses, and we were allowed to take them for the horses. They didn't leave a spear of it. Isn't it pitiful? Everything that the heart of man and woman can devise has been sent out for the "Tommies," but no one thinks of the poor horses. They get the worst of it all the time. Even now we blush to see the handful of hay that each horse gets at a feed.

The Boer War is so far off in time and space that a few further detached references must suffice:

When riding into Bloemfontein met Lord ——'s funeral at the cemetery gates, —— band, firing party, Union Jack, and about three companies. A few yards farther on a "Tommy" covered only by his blanket, escorted by thirteen men all told, the last class distinction that the world can ever make.

We had our baptism of fire yesterday. They opened on us from the left flank. Their first shell was about 150 yards in front — direction good. The next was 100 yards over; and we thought we were bracketed. Some shrapnel burst over us and scattered on all sides. I felt as if a hail storm was coming down, and wanted to turn my back, but it was over in an instant. The whistle of a shell is unpleasant. You hear it begin to scream; the scream grows louder and louder; it seems to be coming exactly your way; then you realize that it has gone over. Most of them fell between our guns and wagons. Our position was quite in the open.

With Ian Hamilton's column near Balmoral.

The day was cold, much like a December day at home, and by my kit going astray I had only light clothing. The rain was fearfully chilly. When we got in about dark we found that the transport could not come up, and it had all our blankets and coats. I had my cape and a rubber sheet for the saddle, both soaking wet. Being on duty I held to camp, the others making for the house nearby where they got poor quarters. I bunked out, supperless like every one else, under an ammunition wagon. It rained most of the night and was bitterly cold. I slept at intervals, keeping the same position all night, both legs in a puddle and my feet being rained on: it was a long night from dark at 5.30 to morning. Ten men in the infantry regiment next us died during the night from exposure. Altogether I never knew such a night, and with decent luck hope never to see such another.

As we passed we saw the Connaughts looking at the graves of their comrades of twenty years ago. The Battery rode at attention and gave "Eyes right": the first time for twenty years that the roll of a British gun has broken in on the silence of those unnamed graves.

We were inspected by Lord Roberts. The battery turned out very smart, and Lord Roberts complimented the Major on its appearance. He then inspected, and afterwards asked to have the officers called out. We were presented to him in turn; he spoke a few words to each of us, asking what our corps and service had been. He seemed surprised that we were all Field Artillery men, but probably the composition of the other Canadian units had to do with this. He asked a good many questions about the horses, the men, and particularly about the spirits of the men. Altogether he showed a very kind interest in the battery.

At nine took the Presbyterian parade to the lines, the first Presbyterian service since we left Canada. We had the right, the Gordons and the Royal Scots next. The music was excellent, led by the brass band of the Royal Scots, which played extremely well. All the singing was from the psalms and paraphrases: "Old Hundred" and "Duke Street" among them. It was very pleasant to hear the old reliables once more. "McCrae's Covenanters" some of the officers called us; but I should not like to set our conduct up against the standard of those austere men.

At Lyndenburg:

The Boers opened on us at about 10,000 yards, the fire being accurate from the first. They shelled us till dark, over three hours. The guns on our left fired for a long time on Buller's camp, the ones on our right on us. We could see the smoke and flash; then there was a soul-consuming interval of 20 to 30 seconds when we would hear the report, and about five seconds later the burst. Many in succession burst over and all around us. I picked up pieces which fell within a few feet. It was a trying afternoon, and we stood around wondering. We moved the horses back, and took cover under the wagons. We were thankful when the sun went down, especially as for the last hour of daylight they turned all their guns on us. The casualties were few.

The next morning a heavy mist prevented the enemy from firing. The division marched out at 7.30 A.M. The attack was made in three columns: cavalry brigade on the left; Buller's troops in the centre, Hamilton's on the right. The Canadian artillery were with Hamilton's division. The approach to the hill was exposed everywhere except where some cover was afforded by ridges. We marched out as support to the Gordons, the cavalry and the Royal Horse Artillery going out to our right as a flank guard. While we were waiting three 100-pound shells struck the top of the ridge in succession about 50 to 75 yards in front of the battery line. We began to feel rather shaky.

On looking over the field at this time one could not tell that anything was occurring except for the long range guns replying to the fire from the hill. The enemy had opened fire as soon as our advance was pushed out. With a glass one could distinguish the infantry pushing up in lines, five or six in succession, the men being some yards apart. Then came a long pause, broken only by the big guns. At last we got the order to advance just as the big guns of the enemy stopped their fire. We advanced about four miles mostly up the slope, which is in all about 1500 feet high, over a great deal of rough ground and over a number of spruits. The horses were put to their utmost to draw the guns up the hills. As we advanced we could see artillery crawling in from both flanks, all converging to the main hill, while far away the infantry and cavalry were beginning to crown the heights near us. Then the field guns and the pompoms began to play. As the field guns came up to a broad plateau section after section came into action, and we fired shrapnel and lyddite on the crests ahead and to the left. Every now and then a rattle of Mausers and Metfords would tell us that the infantry were at their work, but practically the battle was over. From being an infantry attack as expected it was the gunners' day, and the artillery seemed to do excellent work.

General Buller pushed up the hill as the guns were at work, and afterwards General Hamilton; the one as grim as his pictures, the other looking very happy. The wind blew through us cold like ice as we stood on the hill; as the artillery ceased fire the mist dropped over us chilling us to the bone. We were afraid we should have to spend the night on the hill, but a welcome order came sending us back to camp, a distance of five miles by the roads, as Buller would hold the hill, and our force must march south. Our front was over eight miles wide and the objective 1500 feet higher than our camp, and over six miles away. If the enemy had had the nerve to stand, the position could scarcely have been taken; certainly not without the loss of thousands.

For this campaign he received the Queen's Medal with three clasps.

VI
Children and Animals

Through all his life, and through all his letters, dogs and children followed him as shadows follow men. To walk in the streets with him was a slow procession. Every dog and every child one met must be spoken to, and each made answer. Throughout the later letters the names Bonfire and Bonneau occur continually. Bonfire was his horse, and Bonneau his dog.

This horse, an Irish hunter, was given to him by John L. Todd. It was wounded twice, and now lives in honourable retirement at a secret place which need not be disclosed to the army authorities. One officer who had visited the hospital writes of seeing him going about the wards with Bonneau and a small French child following after. In memory of his love for animals and children the following extracts will serve:

You ask if the wee fellow has a name — Mike, mostly, as a term of affection. He has found a cupboard in one ward in which oakum is stored, and he loves to steal in there and "pick oakum," amusing himself as long as is permitted. I hold that this indicates convict ancestry to which Mike makes no defence.

The family is very well, even one-eyed Mike is able to go round the yard in his dressing-gown, so to speak. He is a queer pathetic little beast and Madame has him "hospitalized" on the bottom shelf of the sideboard in the living room, whence he comes down (six inches to the floor) to greet me, and then gravely hirples back, the hind legs looking very pathetic as he hops in. But he is full of spirit and is doing very well.

John McCrae and Bonneau. From a postcard photo taken in Flanders and sent to a friend in Dundas, Ontario.

As to the animals — "those poor voiceless creatures," say you. I wish you could hear them. Bonneau and Mike are a perfect Dignity and Impudence; and both vocal to a wonderful degree. Mike's face is exactly like the terrier in the old picture, and he sits up and gives his paw just like Bonneau, and I never saw him have any instruction; and as for voice, I wish you could hear Bonfire's "whicker" to me in the stable or elsewhere. It is all but talk. There is one ward door that he tries whenever we pass. He turns his head around, looks into the door, and waits. The Sisters in the ward have changed frequently, but all alike "fall for it," as they say, and produce a biscuit or some such dainty which Bonfire takes with much gravity and gentleness. Should I chide him for being too eager and give him my hand saying, "Gentle now," he mumbles with his lips, and licks with his tongue like a dog to show how gentle he can be when he tries. Truly a great boy is that same. On this subject I am like a doting grandmother, but forgive it.

I have a very deep affection for Bonfire, for we have been through so much together, and some of it bad enough. All the hard spots to which one's memory turns the old fellow has shared, though he says so little about it.

This love of animals was no vagrant mood. Fifteen years before in South Africa he wrote in his diary under date of September 11th, 1900:

I wish I could introduce you to the dogs of the force. The genus dog here is essentially sociable, and it is a great pleasure to have them about. I think I have a personal acquaintance with them all. There are our pups — Dolly, whom I always know by her one black and one white eyebrow; Grit and Tory, two smaller gentlemen, about the size of a pound of butter — and fighters; one small white gentleman who rides on a horse, on the blanket; Kitty, the monkey, also rides the off lead of the forge wagon. There is a black almond-eyed person belonging to the Royal Scots, who begins to twist as far as I can see her, and comes up in long curves, extremely genially. A small shaggy chap who belongs to the Royal Irish stands upon his hind legs and spars with his front feet — and lots of others — every one of them "a soldier and a man." The Royal Scots have a monkey, Jenny, who goes around always trailing a sack in her hand, into which she creeps if necessary to obtain shelter.

The other day old Jack, my horse, was bitten by his next neighbor; he turned *slowly*, eyed his opponent, shifted his rope so that he had a little more room, turned very deliberately, and planted both heels in the offender's stomach. He will not be run upon.

From a time still further back comes a note in a like strain. In 1898 he was house physician in a children's hospital at Mt. Airy, Maryland, when he wrote:

A kitten has taken up with a poor cripple dying of muscular atrophy who cannot move. It stays with him all the time, and sleeps most of the day in his straw hat. To-night I saw the kitten curled up under the bed-clothes. It seems as if it were a gift of Providence that the little creature should attach itself to the child who needs it most.

Of another child:

> The day she died she called for me all day, deposed the nurse who was sitting by her, and asked me to remain with her. She had to be held up on account of lack of breath; and I had a tiring hour of it before she died, but it seemed to make her happier and was no great sacrifice. Her friends arrived twenty minutes too late. It seems hard that Death will not wait the poor fraction of an hour, but so it is.

And here are some letters to his nephews and nieces which reveal his attitude both to children and to animals.

From Bonfire to Sergt.-Major Jack Kilgour
August 6th, 1916.
Did you ever have a sore hock? I have one now, and Cruickshank puts bandages on my leg. He also washed my white socks for me. I am glad you got my picture. My master is well, and the girls tell me I am looking well, too. The ones I like best give me biscuits and sugar, and sometimes flowers. One of them did not want to give me some mignonette the other day because she said it would make me sick. It did not make me sick. Another one sends me bags of carrots. If you don't know how to eat carrots, tops and all, you had better learn, but I suppose you are just a boy, and do not know how good oats are.
BONFIRE His ∩ Mark.

From Bonfire to Sergt.-Major Jack Kilgour
October 1st, 1916.

DEAR JACK,

Did you ever eat blackberries? My master and I
pick them every day on the hedges. I like twenty
at a time. My leg is better but I have a lump on my
tummy. I went to see my doctor to-day, and he says
it is nothing at all. I have another horse staying in
my stable now; he is black, and about half my size.
He does not keep me awake at night. Yours truly,
BONFIRE His ∩ Mark.

From Bonfire to Margaret Kilgour, Civilian
November 5th, 1916.

DEAR MARGARET:

This is Guy Fox Day! I spell it that way because
fox-hunting was my occupation a long time ago
before the war. How are Sergt.-Major Jack and
Corporal David? Ask Jack if he ever bites through
his rope at night, and gets into the oat-box. And
as for the Corporal, "I bet you" I can jump as far
as he can. I hear David has lost his red coat. I still
have my grey one, but it is pretty dirty now, for I
have not had a new one for a long time. I got my
hair cut a few weeks ago and am to have new boots
next week. Bonneau and Follette send their love.
Yours truly,

BONFIRE His ∩ Mark.

IN FLANDERS, April 3rd, 1915.

MY DEAR MARGARET:

There is a little girl in this house whose name
is Clothilde. She is ten years old, and calls me
"Monsieur le Major." How would you like it if

twenty or thirty soldiers came along and lived in your house and put their horses in the shed or the stable? There are not many little boys and girls left in this part of the country, but occasionally one meets them on the roads with baskets of eggs or loaves of bread. Most of them have no homes, for their houses have been burnt by the Germans; but they do not cry over it. It is dangerous for them, for a shell might hit them at any time — and it would not be an eggshell, either.

Bonfire is very well. Mother sent him some packets of sugar, and if ever you saw a big horse excited about a little parcel, it was Bonfire. He can have only two lumps in any one day, for there is not much of it. Twice he has had gingerbread and he is very fond of that. It is rather funny for a soldier-horse, is it not? But soldier

John McCrae on his horse, Bonfire.

horses have a pretty hard time of it, sometimes, so we do not grudge them a little luxury. Bonfire's friends are King, and Prince, and Saxonia, — all nice big boys. If they go away and leave him, he whinnies till he catches sight of them again, and then he is quite happy. How is the 15th Street Brigade getting on? Tell Mother I recommend Jack for promotion to corporal if he has been good. David will have to be a gunner for awhile yet, for everybody cannot be promoted. Give my love to Katharine, and Jack, and David.
Your affectionate uncle Jack.

Bonfire, and Bonneau, and little Mike, are all well. Mike is about four months old and has lost an eye and had a leg broken, but he is a very good little boy all the same. He is very fond of Bonfire, and Bonneau, and me. I go to the stable and whistle, and Bonneau and Mike come running out squealing with joy, to go for a little walk with me. When Mike comes to steps, he puts his feet on the lowest steps and turns and looks at me and I lift him up. He is a dear ugly little chap.

The dogs are often to be seen sprawled on the floor of my tent. I like to have them there for they are very home-like beasts. They never seem French to me. Bonneau can "donner la patte" in good style nowadays, and he sometimes curls up inside the rabbit hutch, and the rabbits seem to like him.

I wish you could see the hundreds of rabbits there are here on the sand-dunes; there are also many larks and jackdaws. (These are different from your brother Jack, although they have black faces.) There are herons, curlews, and even ducks; and the other day I saw four young weasels in a heap, jumping over each other from side to side as they ran.

Sir Bertrand Dawson has a lovely little spaniel, Sue, quite black, who goes around with him. I am quite a favourite, and one day Sir Bertrand said to me, "She has brought you a present," and here she was waiting earnestly for me to remove from her mouth a small stone. It is usually a simple gift, I notice, and does not embarrass by its value.

Bonfire is very sleek and trim, and we journey much. If I sit down in his reach I wish you could see how deftly he can pick off my cap and swing it high out of my reach. He also carries my crop; his games are simple, but he does not readily tire of them.

I lost poor old Windy. He was the regimental dog of the 1st Batt. Lincolns, and came to this vale of Avalon to be healed of his second wound. He spent a year at Gallipoli and was "over the top" twice with his battalion. He came to us with his papers like any other patient, and did very well for a while, but took suddenly worse. He had all that care and love could suggest and enough morphine to keep the pain down; but he was very pathetic, and I had resolved that it would be true friendship to help him over when he "went west." He is buried in our woods like any other good soldier, and yesterday I noticed that some one has laid a little wreath of ivy on his grave. He was an old dog evidently, but we are all sore-hearted at losing him. His kit is kept should his master return, — only his collar with his honourable marks, for his wardrobe was of necessity simple. So another sad chapter ends.

September 29th, 1915.

Bonneau gravely accompanies me round the
wards and waits for me, sitting up in a most dig-
nified way. He comes into my tent and sits there
very gravely while I dress. Two days ago a Sister
brought out some biscuits for Bonfire, and not
understanding the rules of the game, which are
bit and bit about for Bonfire and Bonneau, gave
all to Bonfire, so that poor Bonneau sat below
and caught the crumbs that fell. I can see that
Bonfire makes a great hit with the Sisters because
he licks their hands just like a dog, and no crumb
is too small to be gone after.

April, 1917.

I was glad to get back; Bonfire and Bonneau
greeted me very enthusiastically. I had a long long
story from the dog, delivered with uplifted muzzle.
They tell me he sat gravely on the roads a great
deal during my absence, and all his accustomed
haunts missed him. He is back on rounds faithfully.

VII
The Old Land and the New

If one were engaged upon a formal work of biography rather than
a mere essay in character, it would be just and proper to investigate
the family sources from which the individual member is sprung;
but I must content myself within the bounds which I have set,
and leave the larger task to a more laborious hand. The essence of
history lies in the character of the persons concerned, rather than
in the feats which they performed. A man neither lives to himself
nor in himself. He is indissolubly bound up with his stock, and

can only explain himself in terms common to his family; but in doing so he transcends the limits of history, and passes into the realms of philosophy and religion.

The life of a Canadian is bound up with the history of his parish, of his town, of his province, of his country, and even with the history of that country in which his family had its birth. The life of John McCrae takes us back to Scotland. In Canada there has been much writing of history of a certain kind. It deals with events rather than with the subtler matter of people, and has been written mainly for purposes of advertising. If the French made a heroic stand against the Iroquois, the sacred spot is now furnished with an hotel from which a free 'bus runs to a station upon the line of an excellent railway. Maisonneuve fought his great fight upon a place from which a vicious mayor cut the trees which once sheltered the soldier, to make way for a fountain upon which would be raised "historical" figures in concrete stone.

The history of Canada is the history of its people, not of its railways, hotels, and factories. The material exists in written or printed form in the little archives of many a family. Such a chronicle is in possession of the Eckford family which now by descent on the female side bears the honoured names of Gow, and McCrae. John Eckford had two daughters, in the words of old Jamie Young, "the most lovingest girls he ever knew." The younger, Janet Simpson, was taken to wife by David McCrae, 21st January, 1870, and on November 30th, 1872, became the mother of John. To her he wrote all these letters, glowing with filial devotion, which I am privileged to use so freely.

There is in the family a tradition of the single name for the males. It was therefore proper that the elder born should be called Thomas, more learned in medicine, more assiduous in practice, and more weighty in intellect even than the otherwise more highly gifted John. He too is professor of medicine, and co-author of a profound work with his master and relative by marriage — Sir William Osler. Also, he wore the King's uniform and served in the present war.

This John Eckford, accompanied by his two daughters, the mother being dead, his sister, her husband who bore the name of Chisholm, and their numerous children emigrated to Canada, May 28th, 1851, in the ship *Clutha* which sailed from the Broomielaw bound for Quebec. The consort, *Wolfville*, upon which they had originally taken passage, arrived in Quebec before them, and lay in the stream, flying the yellow flag of quarantine. Cholera had broken out. "Be still, and see the salvation of the Lord," were the words of the family morning prayers.

In the *Clutha* also came as passengers James and Mary Gow; their cousin, one Duncan Monach; Mrs. Hanning, who was a sister of Thomas Carlyle; and her two daughters. On the voyage they escaped the usual hardships, and their fare appears to us in these days to have been abundant. The weekly ration was three quarts of water, two ounces of tea, one half pound of sugar, one half pound molasses, three pounds of bread, one pound of flour, two pounds of rice, and five pounds of oatmeal.

The reason for this migration is succinctly stated by the head of the house. "I know how hard it was for my mother to start me, and I wanted land for my children and a better opportunity for them." And yet his parents in their time appear to have "started" him pretty well, although his father was obliged to confess, "I never had more of this world's goods than to bring up my family by the labour of my hands honestly, but it is more than my Master owned, who had not where to lay His head." They allowed him that very best means of education, a calmness of the senses, as he herded sheep on the Cheviot Hills. They put him to the University in Edinburgh, as a preparation for the ministry, and supplied him with ample oatmeal, peasemeal bannocks, and milk. In that great school of divinity he learned the Hebrew, Greek, and Latin; he studied Italian, and French under Surenne, him of blessed memory even unto this day.

John Eckford in 1839 married Margaret Christie, and he went far afield for a wife, namely from Newbigging in Forfar, where for fourteen years he had his one and only charge, to Strathmiglo in Fife. The marriage was fruitful and a happy one, although there is a hint in the record of some religious difference upon which one would like to dwell if the subject were not too esoteric for this generation. The minister showed a certain indulgence, and so long as his wife lived he never employed the paraphrases in the solemn worship of the sanctuary. She was a woman of provident mind. Shortly after they were married he made the discovery that she had prepared the grave clothes for him as well as for herself. Too soon, after only eight years, it was her fate to be shrouded in them. After her death — probably because of her death — John Eckford emigrated to Canada.

To one who knows the early days in Canada there is nothing new in the story of this family. They landed in Montreal July 11th, 1851, forty-four days out from Glasgow. They proceeded by steamer to Hamilton, the fare being about a dollar for each passenger. The next stage was to Guelph; then on to Durham, and finally they came to the end of their journeying near Walkerton in Bruce County in the primeval forest, from which they cut out a home for themselves and for their children.

It was "the winter of the deep snow." One transcription from the record will disclose the scene:

> At length a grave was dug on a knoll in the bush
> at the foot of a great maple with a young snow-
> laden hemlock at the side. The father and the
> eldest brother carried the box along the shovelled
> path. The mother close behind was followed by
> the two families. The snow was falling heavily. At
> the grave John Eckford read a psalm, and prayed,
> "that they might be enabled to believe, the mercy
> of the Lord is from everlasting to everlasting unto
> them that fear Him."

John McCrae himself was an indefatigable church-goer. There is a note in childish characters written from Edinburgh in his thirteenth year, "On Sabbath went to service four times." There the statement stands in all its austerity. A letter from a chaplain is extant in which a certain mild wonder is expressed at the regularity in attendance of an officer of field rank. To his sure taste in poetry the hymns were a sore trial. "Only forty minutes are allowed for the service," he said, "and it is sad to see them 'snappit up' by these poor bald four-line things."

On Easter Sunday, 1915, he wrote: "We had a church parade this morning, the first since we arrived in France. Truly, if the dead rise not, we are of all men the most miserable." On the funeral service of a friend he remarks: "'Forasmuch as it hath pleased Almighty God,' — what a summary of the whole thing that is!" On many occasions he officiated in the absence of the chaplains who in those days would have as many as six services a day. In civil life in Montreal he went to church in the evening, and sat under the Reverend James Barclay of St. Pauls, now designated by some at least as St. Andrews.

VIII
The Civil Years

It will be observed in this long relation of John McCrae that little mention has yet been made of what after all was his main concern in life. For twenty years he studied and practised medicine. To the end he was an assiduous student and a very profound practitioner. He was a student, not of medicine alone, but of all subjects ancillary to the science, and to the task he came with a mind braced by a sound and generous education. Any education of real value a man must have received before he has attained to the age of seven years. Indeed he may be left impervious to its influence at seven weeks. John McCrae's education began well. It began in the time of his two grandfathers at least, was continued by his father and mother before he came upon this world's scene, and by them was left deep founded for him to build upon.

Noble natures have a repugnance from work. Manual labour is servitude. A day of idleness is a holy day. For those whose means do not permit to live in idleness the school is the only refuge; but they must prove their quality. This is the goal which drives many Scotch boys to the University, scorning delights and willing to live long, mind-laborious days.

John McCrae's father felt bound "to give the boy a chance," but the boy must pass the test. The test in such cases is the Shorter Catechism, that compendium of all intellectual argument. How the faithful aspirant for the school acquires this body of written knowledge at a time when he has not yet learned the use of letters is a secret not to be lightly disclosed. It may indeed be that already his education is complete. Upon the little book is always printed the table of multiples, so that the obvious truth which is comprised in the statement, "two by two makes four," is imputed to the contents which are within the cover. In studying the table the catechism is learned surreptitiously, and therefore without self-consciousness.

So, in this well ordered family with its atmosphere of obedience, we may see the boy, like a youthful Socrates going about with a copy of the book in his hand, enquiring of those, who could already read, not alone what were the answers to the questions but the very questions themselves to which an answer was demanded.

This learning, however, was only a minor part of life, since upon a farm life is very wide and very deep. In due time the school was accomplished, and there was a master in the school — let his name be recorded — William Tytler, who had a feeling for English writing and a desire to extend that feeling to others.

In due time also the question of a University arose. There was a man in Canada named Dawson — Sir William Dawson. I have written of him in another place. He had the idea that a university had something to do with the formation of character, and that in the formation of character religion had a part. He was principal of McGill. I am not saying that all boys who entered that University were religious boys when they went in, or even religious men when they came out; but religious fathers had a general desire to place their boys under Sir William Dawson's care.

Those were the days of a queer, and now forgotten, controversy over what was called "Science and Religion." Of that also I have written in another place. It was left to Sir William Dawson to deliver the last word in defence of a cause that was already lost. His book came under the eye of David McCrae, as most books of the time did, and he was troubled in his heart. His boys were at the University of Toronto. It was too late; but he eased his mind by writing a letter. To this letter John replies under date 20th December, 1890: "You say that after reading Dawson's book you almost regretted that we had not gone to McGill. That, I consider, would have been rather a calamity, about as much so as going to Queen's." We are not always wiser than our fathers were, and in the end he came to McGill after all.

For good or ill, John McCrae entered the University of Toronto in 1888, with a scholarship for "general proficiency." He joined the Faculty of Arts, took the honours course in natural sciences, and graduated from the department of biology in 1894, his course having been interrupted by two severe illnesses. From natural science, it was an easy step to medicine, in which he was encouraged by Ramsay Wright, A.B. Macallum, A. McPhedran, and I.H. Cameron. In 1898 he graduated again, with a gold medal, and a scholarship in physiology and pathology. The previous summer he had spent at the Garrett Children's Hospital in Mt. Airy, Maryland.

Upon graduating he entered the Toronto General Hospital as resident house officer; in 1899 he occupied a similar post at Johns Hopkins. Then he came to McGill University as fellow in pathology and pathologist to the Montreal General Hospital. In time he was appointed physician to the Alexandra Hospital for infectious diseases; later assistant physician to the Royal Victoria Hospital, and lecturer in medicine in the University. By examination he became a member of the Royal College of Physicians, London. In 1914 he was elected a member of the Association of American Physicians. These are distinctions won by few in the profession.

In spite, or rather by reason, of his various attainments John McCrae never developed, or degenerated, into the type of the pure scientist. For the laboratory he had neither the mind nor the hands. He never peered at partial truths so closely as to mistake them for the whole truth; therefore, he was unfitted for that purely scientific career which was developed to so high a pitch of perfection in that nation which is now no longer mentioned amongst men. He wrote much, and often, upon medical problems. The papers bearing his name amount to thirty-three items in the catalogues. They testify to his industry rather than to invention and discovery, but they have made his name known in every textbook of medicine.

Apart from his verse, and letters, and diaries, and contributions to journals and books of medicine, with an occasional address to students or to societies, John McCrae left few writings, and in these there is nothing remarkable by reason of thought or expression. He could not write prose. Fine as was his ear for verse he could not produce that finer rhythm of prose, which comes from the fall of proper words in proper sequence. He never learned that if a writer of prose takes care of the sound the sense will take care of itself. He did not scrutinize words to discover their first and fresh meaning. He wrote in phrases, and used words at second-hand as the journalists do. Bullets "rained"; guns "swept"; shells "hailed"; events "transpired," and yet his appreciation of style in others was perfect, and he was an insatiable reader of the best books. His letters are strewn with names of authors whose worth time has proved. To specify them would merely be to write the catalogue of a good library.

The thirteen years with which this century opened were the period in which John McCrae established himself in civil life in Montreal and in the profession of medicine. Of this period he has left a chronicle which is at once too long and too short.

All lives are equally interesting if only we are in possession of all the facts. Places like Oxford and Cambridge have been made interesting because the people who live in them are in the habit of writing, and always write about each other. Family letters have little interest even for the family itself, if they consist merely of a recital of the trivial events of the day. They are prized for the unusual and for the sentiment they contain. Diaries also are dull unless they deal with selected incidents; and selection is the essence of every art. Few events have any interest in themselves, but any event can be made interesting by the pictorial or literary art.

When he writes to his mother, that, as he was coming out of the college, an Irish setter pressed a cold nose against his hand, that is interesting because it is unusual. If he tells us that a professor took him by the arm, there is no interest in that to her or to any one else. For that reason the ample letters and diaries which cover these years need not detain us long. There is in them little selection, little art — too much professor and too little dog.

It is, of course, the business of the essayist to select; but in the present case there is little to choose. He tells of invitations to dinner, accepted, evaded, or refused; but he does not always tell who were there, what he thought of them, or what they had to eat. Dinner at the Adami's, — supper at Ruttan's, — a night with Owen, — tea at the Reford's, — theatre with the Hickson's, — a reception at the Angus's, — or a dance at the Allan's, — these events would all be quite meaningless without an exposition of the social life of Montreal, which is too large a matter to undertake, alluring as the task would be. Even then, one would be giving one's own impressions and not his.

Wherever he lived he was a social figure. When he sat at table the dinner was never dull. The entertainment he offered was not missed by the dullest intelligence. His contribution was merely "stories," and these stories in endless succession were told in a spirit of frank fun. They were not illustrative, admonitory, or hortatory. They were just amusing, and always fresh. This gift he acquired from his mother, who had that rare charm of mimicry without mockery, and caricature without malice. In all his own letters there is not an unkind comment or tinge of ill-nature, although in places, especially in later years, there is bitter indignation against those Canadian patriots who were patriots merely for their bellies' sake.

Taken together his letters and diaries are a revelation of the heroic struggle by which a man gains a footing in a strange place in that most particular of all professions, a struggle comprehended by those alone who have made the trial of it. And yet the method is simple. It is all disclosed in his words, "I have never refused any work that was given me to do." These records are merely a chronicle of work. Outdoor clinics, laboratory tasks, post-mortems, demonstrating, teaching, lecturing, attendance upon the sick in wards and homes, meetings, conventions, papers, addresses, editing, reviewing, — the very remembrance of such a career is enough to appall the stoutest heart.

But John McCrae was never appalled. He went about his work gaily, never busy, never idle. Each minute was pressed into the service, and every hour was made to count. In the first eight months of practice he claims to have made ninety dollars. It is many years before we hear him complain of the drudgery of sending out accounts, and sighing for the services of a bookkeeper. This is the only complaint that appears in his letters.

There were at the time in Montreal two rival schools, and are yet two rival hospitals. But John McCrae was of no party. He was the friend of all men, and the confidant of many. He sought nothing for himself and by seeking not he found what he most desired. His mind was single and his intention pure; his acts unsullied by selfish thought; his aim was true because it was steady and high. His aid was never sought for any cause that was unworthy, and those humorous eyes could see through the bones to the marrow of a scheme. In spite of his singular innocence, or rather by reason of it, he was the last man in the world to be imposed upon.

In all this devastating labour he never neglected the assembling of himself together with those who write and those who paint. Indeed, he had himself some small skill in line and colour. His hands were the hands of an artist — too fine and small for a body that weighted 180 pounds, and measured more than five feet eleven inches in height. There was in Montreal an institution known as "The Pen and Pencil Club." No one now living remembers a time when it did not exist. It was a peculiar club. It contained no member who should not be in it; and no one was left out who should be in. The number was about a dozen. For twenty years the club met in Dyonnet's studio, and afterwards, as the result of some convulsion, in K.R. Macpherson's. A ceremonial supper was eaten once a year, at which one dressed the salad, one made the coffee, and Harris sang a song. Here all pictures were first shown, and writings read — if they were not too long. If they were, there was in an adjoining room a tin chest, which in these austere days one remembers with refreshment. When John McCrae was offered membership he "grabbed at it," and the place was a home for the spirit wearied by the week's work. There Brymner and the other artists would discourse upon writings, and Burgess and the other writers would discourse upon pictures.

It is only with the greatest of resolution, fortified by lack of time and space, that I have kept myself to the main lines of his career, and refrained from following him into by-paths and secret, pleasant places; but I shall not be denied just one indulgence. In the great days when Lord Grey was Governor-General he formed a party to visit Prince Edward Island. The route was a circuitous one. It began at Ottawa; it extended to Winnipeg, down the Nelson River to York Factory, across Hudson Bay, down the Strait, by Belle Isle and Newfoundland, and across the Gulf of St. Lawrence to a place called Orwell. Lord Grey in the matter of company had the reputation of doing himself well. John McCrae was of the party. It also included John Macnaughton, L.S. Amery, Lord Percy, Lord Lanesborough, and one or two others. The ship had called at North Sydney where Lady Grey and the Lady Evelyn joined.

Through the place in a deep ravine runs an innocent stream which broadens out into still pools, dark under the alders. There was a rod — a very beautiful rod in two pieces. It excited his suspicion. It was put into his hand, the first stranger hand that ever held it; and the first cast showed that it was a worthy hand. The sea-trout were running that afternoon. Thirty years before, in that memorable visit to Scotland, he had been taken aside by "an old friend of his grandfather's." It was there he learned "to love the trooties." The love and the art never left him. It was at this same Orwell his brother first heard the world called to arms on that early August morning in 1914.

In those civil years there were, of course, diversions: visits to the United States and meetings with notable men — Welch, Futcher, Hurd, White, Howard, Barker: voyages to Europe with a detailed itinerary upon the record; walks and rides upon the mountain; excursion in winter to the woods, and in summer to the lakes; and one visit to the Packards in Maine, with the sea enthusiastically described. Upon those woodland excursions and upon many other adventures his companion is often referred to as "Billy T.," who can be no other than Lieut.-Col. W.G. Turner, "M.C."

Much is left out of the diary that we would wish to have recorded. There is tantalizing mention of "conversations" with Shepherd — with Roddick — with Chipman — with Armstrong — with Gardner — with Martin — with Moyse. Occasionally there is a note of description: "James Mavor is a kindly genius with much knowledge"; "Tait McKenzie presided ideally" at a Shakespeare dinner; "Stephen Leacock does not keep all the good things for his publisher." Those who know the life in Montreal may well for themselves supply the details.

IX
Dead in His Prime

John McCrae left the front after the second battle of Ypres, and never returned. On June 1st, 1915, he was posted to No. 3 General Hospital at Boulogne, a most efficient unit organized by McGill University and commanded by that fine soldier Colonel H.S. Birkett, C.B. He was placed in charge of medicine, with the rank of Lieut.-Colonel as from April 17th, 1915, and there he remained until his death.

At first he did not relish the change. His heart was with the guns. He had transferred from the artillery to the medical service as recently as the previous autumn, and embarked a few days afterwards at Quebec, on the 29th of September, arriving at Devenport, October 20th, 1914. Although he was attached as Medical Officer to the 1st Brigade of Artillery, he could not forget that he was no longer a gunner, and in those tumultuous days he was often to be found in the observation post rather than in his dressing station. He had inherited something of the old army superciliousness towards a "non-combatant" service, being unaware that in this war the battle casualties in the medical corps were to be higher than in any other arm of the service. From South Africa he wrote exactly fifteen years before: "I am glad that I am not 'a medical' out here. No 'R.A.M.C.' or any other 'M.C.' for me. There is a big breach, and the medicals are on the far side of it." On August 7th, 1915, he writes from his hospital post, "I expect to wish often that I had stuck by the artillery." But he had no choice.

Of this period of his service there is little written record. He merely did his work, and did it well, as he always did what his mind found to do. His health was failing. He suffered from the cold. A year before his death he writes on January 25th, 1917:

The cruel cold is still holding. Everyone is suffering, and the men in the wards in bed cannot keep warm. I know of nothing so absolutely pitiless as weather. Let one wish; let one pray; do what one will; still the same clear sky and no sign, — you know the cold brand of sunshine. For my own part I do not think I have ever been more uncomfortable. Everything is so cold that it hurts to pick it up. To go to bed is a nightmare and to get up a worse one. I have heard of cold weather in Europe, and how the poor suffer, — now I know!

All his life he was a victim of asthma. The first definite attack was in the autumn of 1894, and the following winter it recurred with persistence. For the next five years his letters abound in references to the malady. After coming to Montreal it subsided; but he always felt that the enemy was around the corner. He had frequent periods in bed; but he enjoyed the relief from work and the occasion they afforded for rest and reading.

In January, 1918, minutes begin to appear upon his official file which were of great interest to him, and to us. Colonel Birkett had relinquished command of the unit to resume his duties as Dean of the Medical Faculty of McGill University. He was succeeded by that veteran soldier, Colonel J.M. Elder, C.M.G. At the same time the command of No. 1 General Hospital fell vacant. Lieut.-Colonel McCrae was required for that post; but a higher honour was in store, namely the place of Consultant to the British Armies in the Field. All these events, and the final great event, are best recorded in the austere official correspondence which I am permitted to extract from the files:

From D.M.S. Canadian Contingents. (Major-General C.L. Foster, C.B.). To O.C. No. 3

General Hospital, B.E.F., 13th December, 1917: There is a probability of the command of No. 1 General Hospital becoming vacant. It is requested, please, that you obtain from Lieut.-Col. J. McCrae his wishes in the matter. If he is available, and willing to take over this command, it is proposed to offer it to him.

O.C. No. 3 General Hospital, B.E.F., To D.M.S. Canadian Contingents, 28th December, 1917: Lieut.-Colonel McCrae desires me to say that, while he naturally looks forward to succeeding to the command of this unit, he is quite willing to comply with your desire, and will take command of No. 1 General Hospital at any time you may wish.

D.G.M.S. British Armies in France. To D.M.S. Canadian Contingents, January 2nd, 1918: It is proposed to appoint Lieut.-Colonel J. McCrae, now serving with No. 3 Canadian General Hospital, Consulting Physician to the British Armies in France. Notification of this appointment, when made, will be sent to you in due course.

D.M.S. Canadian Contingents. To O.C. No. 3 General Hospital, B.E.F., January 5th, 1918: Since receiving your letter I have information from G.H.Q. that they will appoint a Consultant Physician to the British Armies in the Field, and have indicated their desire for Lieut.-Colonel McCrae for this duty. This is a much higher honour than commanding a General Hospital, and I hope he will take the post, as this is a

position I have long wished should be filled by
a C.A.M.C. officer.

D.M.S. Canadian Contingents. To D.G.M.S.,
G.H.Q., 2nd Echelon, January 15th, 1918: I
fully concur in this appointment, and con-
sider this officer will prove his ability as an able
Consulting Physician.

Telegram: D.G.M.S., G.H.Q., 2nd Echelon. To
D.M.S. Canadian Contingents, January 18th,
1918: Any objection to Lieut.-Col. J. McCrae
being appointed Consulting Physician to British
Armies in France. If appointed, temporary rank
of Colonel recommended.

Telegram: O.C. No. 3 General Hospital, B.E.F.
To D.M.S. Canadian Contingents, January 27th,
1918: Lieut.-Col. John McCrae seriously ill with
pneumonia at No. 14 General Hospital.

Telegram: O.C. No. 14 General Hospital. To O.C.
No. 3 General Hospital, B.E.F., January 28th, 1918:
Lieut.-Col. John McCrae died this morning.

This was the end. For him the war was finished and all the
glory of the world had passed.

Henceforth we are concerned not with the letters he wrote,
but with the letters which were written about him. They came
from all quarters, literally in hundreds, all inspired by pure sympa-
thy, but some tinged with a curiosity which it is hoped this writing
will do something to assuage.

Let us first confine ourselves to the facts. They are all con-
tained in a letter which Colonel Elder wrote to myself in

common with other friends. On Wednesday, January 23rd, he was as usual in the morning; but in the afternoon Colonel Elder found him asleep in his chair in the mess room. "I have a slight headache," he said. He went to his quarters. In the evening he was worse, but had no increase of temperature, no acceleration of pulse or respiration. At this moment the order arrived for him to proceed forthwith as Consulting Physician of the First Army. Colonel Elder writes, "I read the order to him, and told him I should announce the contents at mess. He was very much pleased over the appointment. We discussed the matter at some length, and I took his advice upon measures for carrying on the medical work of the unit."

Next morning he was sleeping soundly, but later on he professed to be much better. He had no fever, no cough, no pain. In the afternoon he sent for Colonel Elder, and announced that he had pneumonia. There were no signs in the chest; but the microscope revealed certain organisms which rather confirmed the diagnosis. The temperature was rising. Sir Bertrand Dawson was sent for. He came by evening from Wimereux, but he could discover no physical signs. In the night the temperature continued to rise, and he complained of headache. He was restless until the morning, "when he fell into a calm, untroubled sleep."

Next morning, being Friday, he was removed by ambulance to No. 14 General Hospital at Wimereux. In the evening news came that he was better; by the morning the report was good, a lowered temperature and normal pulse. In the afternoon the condition grew worse; there were signs of cerebral irritation with a rapid, irregular pulse; his mind was quickly clouded. Early on Sunday morning the temperature dropped, and the heart grew weak; there was an intense sleepiness. During the day the sleep increased to coma, and all knew the end was near.

His friends had gathered. The choicest of the profession was there, but they were helpless. He remained unconscious, and died at half past one on Monday morning. The cause of death was double pneumonia with massive cerebral infection. Colonel Elder's letter concludes: "We packed his effects in a large box, everything that we thought should go to his people, and Gow took it with him to England to-day." Walter Gow was his cousin, a son of that Gow who sailed with the Eckfords from Glasgow in the *Clutha*. At the time he was Deputy Minister in London of the Overseas Military Forces of Canada. He had been sent for but arrived too late; — all was so sudden.

The funeral was held on Tuesday afternoon, January 29th, at the cemetery in Wimereux. The burial was made with full military pomp. From the Canadian Corps came Lieut.-General Sir Arthur Currie, the General Officer Commanding; Major-General E.W.B. Morrison, and Brigadier-General W.O.H. Dodds, of the Artillery. Sir A.T. Sloggett, the Director-General of Medical Services, and his Staff were waiting at the grave. All Commanding Officers at the Base, and all Deputy Directors were there. There was also a deputation from the Harvard Unit headed by Harvey Cushing.

Bonfire went first, led by two grooms, and decked in the regulation white ribbon, not the least pathetic figure in the sad procession. A hundred nursing Sisters in caps and veils stood in line, and then proceeded in ambulances to the cemetery, where they lined up again. Seventy-five of the personnel from the Hospital acted as escort, and six Sergeants bore the coffin from the gates to the grave. The firing party was in its place. Then followed the chief mourners, Colonel Elder and Sir Bertrand Dawson; and in their due order, the rank and file of No. 3 with their officers; the rank and file of No. 14 with their officers; all officers from the Base, with Major-General Wilberforce and the Deputy Directors to complete.

It was a springtime day, and those who have passed all those winters in France and in Flanders will know how lovely the springtime may be. So we may leave him, "on this sunny slope, facing the sunset and the sea." These are the words used by one of the nurses in a letter to a friend, — those women from whom no heart is hid. She also adds:"The nurses lamented that he became unconscious so quickly they could not tell him how much they cared. To the funeral all came as we did, because we loved him so."

At first there was the hush of grief and the silence of sudden shock. Then there was an outbreak of eulogy, of appraisement, and sorrow. No attempt shall be made to reproduce it here; but one or two voices may be recorded in so far as in disjointed words they speak for all. Stephen Leacock, for those who write, tells of his high vitality and splendid vigour — his career of honour and marked distinction — his life filled with honourable endeavour and instinct with the sense of duty — a sane and equable temperament — whatever he did, filled with sure purpose and swift conviction.

Dr. A.D. Blackader, acting Dean of the Medical Faculty of McGill University, himself speaking from out of the shadow, thus appraises his worth: "As a teacher, trusted and beloved; as a colleague, sincere and cordial; as a physician, faithful, cheerful, kind. An unkind word he never uttered." Oskar Klotz, himself a student, testifies that the relationship was essentially one of master and pupil. From the head of his first department at McGill, Professor, now Colonel, Adami, comes the weighty phrase, that he was sound in diagnosis; as a teacher inspiring; that few could rise to his high level of service.

There is yet a deeper aspect of this character with which we are concerned; but I shrink from making the exposition, fearing lest with my heavy literary tread I might destroy more than I should discover. When one stands by the holy place wherein dwells a dead friend's soul — the word would slip out at last — it becomes him to take off the shoes from off his feet. But fortunately the dilemma does not arise. The task has already been performed by one who by God has been endowed with the religious sense, and by nature enriched with the gift of expression;

one who in his high calling has long been acquainted with the grief of others, and is now himself a man of sorrow, having seen with understanding eyes,

> These great days range like tides,
> And leave our dead on every shore.

On February 14th, 1918, a Memorial Service was held in the Royal Victoria College. Principal Sir William Peterson presided. John Macnaughton gave the address in his own lovely and inimitable words, to commemorate one whom he lamented, "so young and strong, in the prime of life, in the full ripeness of his fine powers, his season of fruit and flower bearing. He never lost the simple faith of his childhood. He was so sure about the main things, the vast things, the indispensable things, of which all formulated faiths are but a more or less stammering expression, that he was content with the rough embodiment in which his ancestors had laboured to bring those great realities to bear as beneficent and propulsive forces upon their own and their children's minds and consciences. His instinctive faith sufficed him."

To his own students John McCrae once quoted the legend from a picture, to him "the most suggestive picture in the world": What I spent I had: what I saved I lost: what I gave I have; — and he added: "It will be in your power every day to store up for yourselves treasures that will come back to you in the consciousness of duty well done, of kind acts performed, things that having given away freely you yet possess. It has often seemed to me that when in the Judgement those surprised faces look up and say, Lord, when saw we Thee anhungered and fed Thee; or thirsty and gave Thee drink; a stranger, and took Thee in; naked and clothed Thee; and there meets them that warrant-royal of all charity, Inasmuch as ye did it unto one of the least of these, ye have done it unto Me, there will be amongst those awed ones many a practitioner of medicine."

And finally I shall conclude this task to which I have set a worn but willing hand, by using again the words which once I used before: Beyond all consideration of his intellectual attainments John McCrae was the well beloved of his friends. He will be missed in his place; and wherever his companions assemble there will be for them a new poignancy in the Miltonic phrase,

> But O the heavy change, now thou art gone,
> Now thou art gone, and never must return!

LONDON,
11th November, 1918.

NOTES

1. Isandlwana was the site of a major defeat in 1879 of parts of the British Army engaged in the invasion of Zululand in South Africa during the Anglo-Zulu war. Over a thousand British soldiers armed with breech-loading rifles were killed by a large force of Zulu warriors armed with assegai spears and cowhide shields.

2. George Frederic Watts (1817–1904), known as the Michelangelo of British painting, was a prominent and popular painter and sculptor of the Victorian Age. Seen as someone with Symbolist inclinations, he was very much an independent spirit who excelled at portraiture and paintings with a strong allegorical and/or narrative element. He was married briefly to the celebrated British actress Ellen Terry (1847–1928), who was thirty years his junior, and married him when she was barely seventeen. In 1897 Watts donated a painting he called "Sic Transit," considered one of his masterworks, to the Tate Gallery. It is a philosophical and contemplative work on the folly of human ambition, hence "sic transit gloria mundi." Watts died in 1904, the same year McCrae published his poem after a study trip to London. A large selection of Watts' paintings are housed in the National Portrait Gallery and the Tate Gallery in London.

3. Sir Andrew Macphail (1864–1938) was born in Prince Edward Island and educated at Prince of Wales College and McGill University in Montreal, where he lived and worked almost his entire life. Trained as a medical doctor, he was Professor of the History of Medicine at McGill, and saw service in the First World War. Macphail was also deeply interested in literature and authored a number of collections of philosophical essays, fiction and religious works. He was founding editor of the University Magazine (1901–1920), in which many of McCrae's poems appeared. He was knighted in 1920.

MORE VOYAGUER CLASSICS BOOKS

A Tangled Web
By L.M. Montgomery
Introduction by Benjamin Lefebvre

No amount of drama between the Dark and Penhallow families can prepare them for what follows when Aunt Becky bequeaths her prized heirloom jug — the owner to be revealed in one year's time. The intermarriages, and resulting fighting and feuding, that have occurred over the years grow more intense as Gay Penhallow's fiancé leaves her for the devious Nan Penhallow; Peter Penhallow and Donna Dark find love after a lifelong hatred of each other; and Joscelyn and Hugh Dark, inexplicably separated on their wedding night, are reunited.

Hopes and shortcomings are revealed as we follow the fates of the clan for an entire year. The legendary jug sits amid this love, heartbreak, and hilarity as each family member works to acquire the heirloom. But on the night that the eccentric matriarch's wishes are to be revealed, both families find the biggest surprise of all.

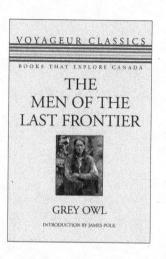

VOYAGEUR CLASSICS

BOOKS THAT EXPLORE CANADA

THE
MEN OF THE
LAST FRONTIER

GREY OWL

INTRODUCTION BY JAMES POLK

The Men of the Last Frontier
By Grey Owl
Introduction by James Polk

In 1931 Grey Owl published his first book, *The Men of the Last Frontier*, a work that is part memoir, part history of the vanishing wilderness in Canada, and part compendium of animal and First Nations tales and lore. A passionate, compelling appeal for the protection and preservation of the natural environment pervades Grey Owl's words and makes his literary debut still ring with great relevance in the 21st century.

By the 1920s, Canada's outposts of adventure had been thrust farther and farther north to the remote margins of the country. Lumbermen, miners, and trappers invaded the primeval forests, seizing on nature's wealth with soulless efficiency. Grey Owl himself fled before the assault as he witnessed his valleys polluted with sawmills, his hills dug up for hidden treasure, and wildlife, particularly his beloved beavers, exterminated for quick fortunes.

Combat Journal for Place d'Armes: A Personal Narrative
By Scott Symons
Introduction by Christopher Elson

Originally published in 1967, *Combat Journal for Place d'Armes*, set in Montreal, was initially met with shock and anger by most reviewers. As D.H. Lawrence's *Lady Chatterley's Lover* once had, it challenged the attitudes and morals held by most people in its time regarding life and literature. Despite this initial reaction, the novel earned author Scott Symons the Beta Sigma Phi Best First Canadian Novel Award and went on to be regarded as one of the "most important statements about Canadian imaginative life in the 1960s."

Both a study of the emergence of a character's true self through his homosexual experiences and his critical examination of Canadian, and especially French-Canadian, culture and traditions, *Place d'Armes* was named one of the top hundred most important books in Canadian history. Peter Buitenhuis, the late author and former head of Simon Fraser University's English department, has written that Symons' novel is "a defiant assault on the Canadian Bourgeois mentality" that "celebrates human sexuality and spirtuality with all the gusto that language can command."

DUNDURN

Visit us at
Dundurn.com
@dundurnpress
Facebook.com/dundurnpress